Pan Study Aids

D0263173

French

C. Beswick, P. J. Downes
illustrations by Jan Pickett

Pan Books London and Sydney
in association with **Heinemann Educational Books**

First published 1980 by Pan Books Ltd,
Cavaye Place, London SW10 9PG
in association with Heinemann Educational Books Ltd
9 8 7 6 5
ISBN 0 330 26113 4
© C. Beswick, P. J. Downes, 1980
Printed and bound in Great Britain by
Richard Clay (The Chaucer Press) Ltd, Bungay, Suffolk

Pan Study Aids

Titles published in this series

Accounts and Book-keeping
Biology
British Government and Politics
Chemistry
Commerce
Economics
Effective Study Skills
English Language
French
Geography 1   *Physical and Human*
Geography 2   *British Isles, Western Europe, North America*
German
History 1   *British*
History 2   *European*
Human Biology
Maths
Physics
Spanish

Brodie's Notes on English Literature

This long established series published in Pan Study Aids now contains
more than 150 titles. Each volume covers one of the major works of
English literature regularly set for examinations.

Contents

Acknowledgements

The publishers are grateful to the following Exam Boards, whose addresses are listed on pages 7 and 8, for permission to reproduce questions from examination papers:

Associated Examining Board, University of Cambridge Local Examinations Syndicate, Joint Matriculation Board, University of London Schools Examination Board, Oxford Delegacy of Local Examinations, Scottish Certificate of Education Examining Board, Southern University Joint Board, Welsh Joint Education Committee.

The suggested answers to past examination questions are the work of the authors and not of the examination boards concerned.

The publishers are also grateful to Hodder and Stoughton Educational for permission to reproduce material from *Le Français d'Aujourd'hui*.

To the student

How this book can help you

Many candidates for O level French are unsure about *what* to revise and *how* to revise most efficiently: this book aims to help with this twin problem. It provides material for vocabulary and grammar revision, broken down into small, manageable units, concentrating on the basic necessities rather than trying to include every possible point. There are regular opportunities for self-testing on vocabulary and grammar. Hints on the techniques of revision are carefully explained. Advice on tackling essay writing, prose composition, comprehensions, translation, oral tests and dictation is given, accompanied by appropriate practice materials. In short there is a variety of guided revision activities for you to do at home.

How to use the study guide
Detailed advice on approach is given at the beginning of major sections of the book, but the following general hints may be helpful.

1 You do not have to work through the book in any special order so it is most important that you should keep a written record of what you revise and your method. (Example – '23 November. Vocab. page 26; learned all words from French to English; words in bold type from English to French; tested myself in writing.')

2 Work in short, sharp bursts in which you really concentrate, rather than very long sessions where half of your concentration is on the television and half on French. A little, often, is a good idea.

3 Revision has to be a lot more than staring at the book. There has to be some activity – ask a friend or relative to test you; you can at least say the word and spell it out even if the person testing you doesn't know any French. Test yourself in writing. Rather than just read a series of hints hoping you'll remember them, shut the book and try

summarizing them. Use a cassette tape recorder to record some of your oral work.

4 Vary your revision activity so you don't get bored. You have a choice of vocabulary work, grammar work (including finding out the meaning of technical terms such as pronouns and auxiliary verbs), verb-table work and practice on five major examination techniques. Frequent, varied work on all these, spread over a whole year rather than left until the last minute, should bring you confident, steady progress.

5 Begin by testing your concentration now: close the book and jot down the four important points of advice that have just been made. *Bon courage!*

The Exam Boards

The addresses given below are those from which copies of syllabuses and past examination papers may be ordered. The abbreviations (AEB, etc) are those used in this book to identify actual questions.

Associated Examining Board, (AEB)
Wellington House,
Aldershot, Hants GU11 1BQ

University of Cambridge Local Examinations Syndicate, (CAM)
Syndicate Buildings, 17 Harvey Road,
Cambridge CB1 2EU

Joint Matriculation Board (JMB)
(Agent) John Sherratt and Son Ltd,
78 Park Road
Altrincham, Cheshire WA14 5QQ

University of London School Examinations Department, (LOND)
66–72 Gower Street.
London WC1E 6EE

Northern Ireland Schools Examination Council (NI)
Examinations Office,
Beechill House,
Beechill Road,
Belfast BT8 4RS

Oxford Delegacy of Local Examinations, (OX)
Ewert Place,
Summertown,
Oxford OX2 7BZ

Scottish Certificate of Education Examining Board,   (SCE)
(Agent) Robert Gibson and Sons, Ltd,
17 Fitzroy Place,
Glasgow G3 7SF

Southern Universities Joint Board,   (SUJB)
Cotham Road, Bristol BS6 6DD

Welsh Joint Education Committee,   (WEL)
245 Western Avenue,
Cardiff CF5 2YX

1 Revising grammar

The grammar section has been divided into small units so that you can work intensively for a short period on a single topic, then test yourself using the practice sentences. Don't forget the need to make revision active (see p5). You need not work in any particular order of units, but keep a diary of *what* and *how* you revise.

In this book we have concentrated on the really important points of grammar which we consider to be a *minimum* requirement: it is essential therefore that you learn these points with complete accuracy. Equally, in the verb tables we have concentrated on the verbs it is essential for you to know if you are to pass the examination. Revise, then test yourself orally and in writing, working on one small group of verbs at a time.

Students often find the grammatical terms which they come across in the classroom or in textbooks rather confusing. The following glossary is intended to give you helpful explanations rather than precise definitions. Grammatical terminology avoids having to repeat explanations several times and you will find some of these terms used in this book too, in order to save space.

Glossary of grammar terms

Noun, proper noun, pronoun

A noun (1) is a word which can make sense with *a* or *the* in front of it; a proper noun (2) is the name of a person or a place, and a pronoun (3) is a word which stands for a noun like *I, you, they*:

(1) the *policeman* arrests the young man
(2) *John* saw the bike
(3) *I* wept

When they are used in a sentence in front of a verb they are referred to as the *subject* of that sentence (see the three examples above).

Verb
A verb is a word which denotes actions, states or happenings:

he *was playing* football
I *am happy* here
it *started* earlier on

Tense
The tense of a verb is the form taken by that verb to indicate the time of the action/state/happening:

present tense   he arrest*s*
imperfect tense   he *was* arrest*ing*
future tense   he *will* arrest

Auxiliary verb
Many past tenses need an auxiliary or helping verb. In the English sentences below the auxiliary verb is a part of *to have*:

I *have* finished
he *has* begun
they *had* arrived

In French the auxiliary verb for the perfect tense is either part of *avoir* or *être*. The spelling of avoir and être alters according to (or agrees with) the subject: j'*ai* fini, tu *as* fini; je *suis* arrivé, tu *es* arrivé etc.

The past participle
The past participle is that part of a verb which helps to form tenses. The English past participle usually ends in *-ed, -d, -t, -en, -n* (vot*ed*, hear*d*, learn*t*, chos*en*, throw*n*): I have *voted*, he has *chosen*, they had *thrown*.

With être verbs the past participle also agrees with the subject, taking extra *-e, -s,* or *-es* according to gender (masculine or feminine word) and number (one, singular; more than one, plural) of the subject: elle est arrivé*e*, ils sont arrivé*s*, elles sont arrivé*es*.

Finite verb
The finite verb is the main verb of a sentence which has *person, number* and *tense*:

ils *ont* dû trouver une solution
nous *avons* dû trouver une solution

Infinitive

The infinitive is the simplest form of the verb, normally preceded *in English only* by *to*, e.g. to work (travailler), to find (trouver), to talk (parler) and it is the form in which most verbs are printed in dictionaries, word lists etc. The most common endings for French infinitives are *-er*, *-ir* or *-re*. An infinitive cannot normally stand on its own in a sentence, there must also be a finite verb in the sentence:

il est difficile de *parler* chinois
je voudrais *faire* une croisière

Note that the infinitive of the verb does *not* change according to subject:
Nous voudrions *faire* une croisière

Adjectives

Adjectives describe nouns or proper nouns:

John read his *new* book

Adverbs

Adverbs describe how an action is performed:

the train moved off *slowly*

Other technical terms

Regular verbs Verbs which follow a predictable pattern according to whether they are of the *-er*, *-ir* or *-re* type (e.g. je donn*e*, tu donn*es*, il donn*e*).

Irregular verbs Verbs which follow an unpredictable pattern which has to be learned for each separate verb (avoir: j'*ai*, tu *as*, il *a*, nous *avons* etc).

Verb ending and verb stem The ending means the letters added to the verb according to the subject (e.g. je fin*is*, tu fin*is*, il fin*it*, nous fin*issons*). The stem is the part of the verb to which these endings are added. The future tense of avoir (j'aur*ai*, tu aur*as*, il aur*a*, nous aur*ons*, vous aur*ez*, ils aur*ont*) consists of stem *aur* + ending *-ai*, *-as*, *-a*, *-ons*, *-ez*, *-ont*.

Gender Nouns in French are either masculine gender or feminine gender. In the case of people, the sex will generally correspond with the gender of the noun – *un* homme; *une* femme. In the case of objects, you have to learn the French gender – *un* crayon; *une* table. Associate firmly in your mind the grammatical equation *un/le* = masculine; *une/la* = feminine.

Preposition A word like *on, in, under, to, at, from, with, without, for,* often followed by a noun or pronoun.

Comparative Big*ger* than ... small*er* than, *more* intelligent than ... *less* intelligent than ...

Superlative The big*gest*, the small*est*, *least* intelligent, happ*iest*.

Positive and negative The following statements are marked (P) for positive and (N) for negative:

I've been to Japan (P)	I've not been to Japan (N)
he is clever (P)	he isn't clever (N)

Affirmative and interrogative The following statements are marked (A) for affirmative and (I) for interrogative:

he is not a good teacher (A)	he's not a good teacher, is he? (I)
I'm happy (A)	am I happy? (I)

Direct and indirect speech In the following statements, the first sentence is in direct speech and the second in indirect:

He said to John, 'Come to my office immediately.'
He said that John was to come to his office immediately.

Idiomatic and word for word translation Remember to be idiomatic in your translations and not to translate word for word:

	idiomatic	*word for word*
faire d'une pierre deux coups	to kill two birds with one stone	to make of one stone two blows
il fait du vent	it's windy	it makes some wind
j'ai onze ans	I'm eleven years old	I have eleven years

Context You can often guess the meaning of a word from the 'surroundings' in which it is found. 'Merry — and a Happy New Year': it is easy to guess from the context of this sentence that the missing word must be *Christmas*.

Verbs

This grammar reference section starts with verbs and their tenses, something crucial to *every* part of the examination.

One of the key tenses is the perfect tense. You use it to express what you, or somebody else, *have done* and what *happened* to you, or somebody else, in the different steps of a story. However, do remember to use the imperfect tense for saying what you *were doing*, what you *used to do* or what things or people *were like*.

The sections that follow deal with verbs which require être in forming their perfect tense, the perfect tense of reflexive verbs and verbs which take avoir as an auxiliary. When you have worked through them all, the flow chart below should make sense. It shows the process which your brain ought to go through before saying or writing a verb in the perfect tense. *Memorize it*, so that you can write it all out without looking at the page. Apply it and you will find you are no longer making any mistakes in the perfect tense!

Être verbs

1 It is vital to be able to use the *être* verbs without mistakes in the perfect tense in all parts of the examination.

2 Many students find it difficult to *remember* which are the key *être* verbs. Use this page to help you memorize them. Fortunately there aren't very many!

3 Study the table below, then work on the test sentences for practice. You should aim to be able to translate out of and into French, with either column covered.

aller to go	venir to come (devenir to become; revenir to come back)	
passer to pass by	arriver to arrive	partir to depart
entrer to enter	rentrer to get back home	sortir to go out
rester to remain, to stay	retourner to go back	tomber to fall
monter to go up	descendre to go down	naître to be born
mourir to die		

Nous sommes allés au café.	We went to the pub.
Sa mère est venue aussi.	Her mother came too.
Nous sommes revenus à mon appartement.	We came back to my flat.
Je suis passé la voir le lendemain.	I dropped in on her (literally: I passed by to see her) the day after.
Il est passé devant l'église.	He passed by the church.
Les agents sont arrivés juste à temps.	The police arrived just in time.
Je suis parti à la hâte.	I left in a hurry.
Le train est parti de la gare.	The train left the station.
Nous sommes entrés dans la boîte de nuit.	We went into the night-club.
Il est sorti sans payer.	He went out without paying.
Sa mère est restée chez elle.	Her mother stayed at home.
Je suis retourné à une heure du matin.	I got back at one a.m.
Elle est tombée dans la gadoue.	She fell in the slush.
Je suis monté à pied.	I went up on foot.
Il est monté dans le train.	He got on the train.

Elle est descendue en ascenseur.	She came down by lift.
Nous sommes descendus de la voiture.	We got out of the car.
Elle est née orpheline.	She was born an orphan.
Elle est morte riche et fameuse.	She died rich and notorious.

Forming the perfect tense of être verbs

1 Once you know which verbs take *être*, concentrate on this page on practice in using them in all persons. Use the correct part of the present tense of *être* for *je, tu, il* etc.
2 Follow with the past participle of the verb you are saying or writing in the perfect tense.
3 Make the past participle agree in gender and number with the person, remembering that *je* and *tu* can be masculine or feminine but must be singular, *vous* can be masculine or feminine, singular or plural, and *nous* can be masculine or feminine but must be plural.
4 Study the test sentences for practice. You should aim to be able to translate out of and into French, with either column covered.

Les garçons sont partis de bonne heure.	The boys left in good time.
'Tu es arrivée à quelle heure, Monique?'	'What time did you arrive, Monique?'
Mes amis et moi sommes allés à la piscine.	My friends and I went to the swimming pool.
La dame est passée devant la banque.	The lady passed by the bank.
'Vous êtes restée chez vous, mademoiselle?'	'Did you stay at home, Miss?'
Les deux sœurs sont mortes il y a deux ans.	The two sisters died two years ago.
L'homme est monté dans sa voiture.	The man got into his car.
Jacqueline est venue en Angleterre.	Jacqueline came to England.
Les deux soldats sont sortis de la caserne.	The two soldiers left the barracks.
Je suis monté sur mon vélo devant la gare.	I got on to my bike outside the station.

Translate into French **1** Prince Charles was born in 1945. **2** She got on her bike. **3** I left Paris (use partir) one year ago. **4** The two girls went to France. **5** The two policeman got off the train. **6** The thief went out of the supermarket. **7** I stayed at home. **8** The two soldiers entered the barracks.

The perfect tense of reflexive verbs

1 A reflexive verb is one which is printed in a word list or dictionary with *se* or *s'* in front of the word. The action of the verb usually 'reflects back' on to the subject of the sentence.

2 All reflexive verbs take *être* in the perfect tense.

3 *Me, t', s', nous, vous, se* come immediately before the correct part of *être* for *je, tu, il/elle, nous, vous, ils/elles*.

4 The rules of agreement for *être* verbs normally apply, with *-e, -s* or *-es* on the end of the past participle.

5 Do not make the mistake of writing all verbs as though they were reflexive. You need to know very few reflexives in your examination tests: the most important ones are listed below.

se réveiller	to wake up
se lever	to get/stand up
se laver	to get washed
se raser	to shave
se dépêcher	to hurry
s'habiller	to get dressed
se reposer	to rest
se coucher	to go to bed
se sauver	to run away

Learn these verbs by working on the test sentences for practice. You should aim to be able to translate out of and into French, with either column covered.

Je me suis réveillé à onze heures ce matin-là.	I woke up at eleven o'clock that morning.
'Tu t'es levée à quelle heure, Françoise?'	'What time did you get up, Françoise?'
Le gosse s'est lavé à contrecœur.	The kid washed reluctantly.
La jeune fille s'est habillée à la hâte.	The girl got dressed in a hurry.
M. Clousot s'est rasé en écoutant la radio.	Mr Clousot shaved whilst listening to the radio.

Nous nous sommes dépêchés de prendre un taxi.	We hurried to catch a taxi.
'Vous vous êtes reposé, monsieur?'	'Did you have a rest, sir?'
M. et Mme Weiss se sont couchés tard.	Mr and Mrs Weiss went to bed late.
Les deux voleurs se sont sauvés.	The two thieves ran away.

Translate into French 1 They woke up at seven-thirty that morning. **2** Mrs Janvier got up straightaway. **3** Then she washed. **4** He got dressed whilst listening to his wife. **5** The man shaved in a hurry. **6** The two girls hurried to arrive at eight o'clock. **7** I had a rest that morning. **8** The children went to bed at midnight. **9** The girls ran away when they saw the man in the park.

The perfect tense of avoir verbs

1 Use *avoir* to form the perfect tense of verbs which are *not* reflexive and *not* part of the *être* group.
2 Deal with regular verbs in the following way:

donn*er* (to give)   j'*ai donné* I have given, I gave
fin*ir* (to finish)   nous *avons fini* we've finished, we finished
vend*re* (to sell)   elle *a vendu* she has sold, she sold

3 The perfect tense column of the verb tables gives you the past participles of the important irregular verbs. Some examples:

condu*ire* (to drive)   ils ont condu*it* they have driven, they drove
rece*voir* (to receive)   tu as re*çu* you've received, you received
voir (to see)   vous avez *vu* you've seen, you saw

4 With *avoir* verbs there is normally no extra -*e*, -*s* or -*es* on the past participle.
5 You will find you need to use a relatively small number of verbs over and over again when talking or writing in the past tense. By careful and regular revision of your verb tables you should *eventually* reach the stage where you can do all the test sentences below without making any mistakes in your translation.

Translate into French **1** They ate their sandwiches. **2** I telephoned my father. **3** She ran to the police station. **4** I drank a cup of coffee. **5** They had to leave the hotel. **6** He finished his work. **7** The teacher punished the two pupils. **8** The waiter filled the glass. **9** She brought a present. **10** He slept for eight hours. **11** They said goodbye to their father. **12** The two boys disappeared. **13** He wrote his name and address. **14** He lost his wallet. **15** They sold their house. **16** I heard a noise. **17** The pupil made a mistake in his homework. **18** Their mother read the postcard. **19** They put the basket in the boot of the car. **20** She opened the window. **21** She offered a tip. **22** It rained last Wednesday. **23** I managed (was able) to run away. **24** He took his umbrella. **25** He followed the thief. **26** I saw the film on television. **27** Their mother drove the car to the station. **28** The girl received a reward. **29** He listened to the radio for half an hour. **30** They found a box in the attic.

Être verbs which sometimes take avoir

1 Don't be too surprised if you sometimes see one of the *être* group of verbs taking *avoir* in the perfect tense. Study these examples:

Elle *a descendu* l'escalier.	She went down the stairs.
J'*ai descendu* ma valise.	I brought down my case.
Tu *as monté* les marches.	You went up the steps.
Elle *a monté* sa malle.	She took her trunk up.
Il *a sorti* son mouchoir.	He got out his handkerchief.
Vous *avez passé* le sel.	You passed the salt.

2 When these verbs have a direct object, as in the sentences above, they take avoir in the perfect tense. This means there will be no extra -*e*, -*s* or -*es* on the past participle.

3 When the verbs in the list above have no object, or when they are followed by a word like *de*, *en*, *dans*, *sur*, *par*, *à* they take être, with agreements on the past participle, as you have already learned.

Elle *est montée*.	She went up(stairs).
Nous *sommes descendus*.	We went down(stairs).
Je *suis descendu* du train.	I got off the train.
Elles *sont sorties* de l'église.	They went out of the church.
Je *suis passé* devant l'église.	I passed by the church.

Translate into French (concentrating on whether the verb should take avoir or être in the perfect) **1** I went out at midnight. **2** He passed by the bus station. **3** She got on her motorbike. **4** He brought down his briefcase. **5** I passed the bottle to him. **6** They went down. **7** We went out of the church. **8** He took his biro out. **9** He went up the steps. **10** They went upstairs.

The imperfect tense

1 An easy tense to form. Take the *nous* form of the present tense of the verb as your starting point.

2 Take off the *-ons* ending and add on the following endings:

je *-ais*   nous *-ions*
tu *-ais*   vous *-iez*
il *-ait*   ils   *-aient*

3 There is only one exception to this rule – the verb *être*: j'étais, tu étais, il était, nous étions, etc.

4 When translating, don't be fooled by the English sentence, 'I was listening to the radio.' The English imperfect has two parts (*was* + listen*ing*). The French imperfect is contained in *one* word – j'*écoutais* la radio.

5 The imperfect is used when talking or writing about: how people or things looked or felt; what used to happen as a rule; what was happening at the time.

Study these test sentences for practice. You should aim to be able to translate out of and into French with either column covered.

Le jeune homme était très impoli.	The young man was most impolite.
La maison était vide.	The house was empty.
Elle portait un nouveau jean.	She was wearing a new pair of jeans.
Les deux garçons avaient peur.	The two boys were scared.
Quand j'avais six ans, je me couchais à sept heures.	When I was six years old, I used to go to bed at seven o'clock.
Je prenais toujours un autobus.	I always used to go by bus.
Il fumait quand le professeur est entré.	He was smoking when the teacher came in.
Il travaillait quand le téléphone a sonné.	He was working when the telephone rang.

Je regardais la télévision quand nos invités sont arrivés.	I was watching the television when our guests arrived.

Translate into French 1 I used to live in Birmingham. 2 She was tired after the journey. 3 The flat was empty. 4 He was holding a gun in his hand. 5 She wore black shoes. 6 They were listening to the radio when they heard a noise. 7 They were hungry. 8 The boy was pleased with his reward. 9 He always went to bed at ten o'clock. 10 They were running away when the police arrived.

The pluperfect tense

1 You will need to use this tense in some of your examination tests and to recognize it when you see it printed or hear it.

2 It is a very easy tense to form once you have mastered the perfect.

3 Its meaning in English is 'had arrived', 'had done' etc.

4 Follow exactly all the rules you have learned for forming the perfect tense but instead of putting the part of avoir or être in the *present* tense, j'ai, tu as, il a, je suis, tu es, il est, write avoir or être in the *imperfect*:
j'avais, tu avais, il avait, nous avions, vous aviez, ils avaient
j'étais, tu étais, il était, nous étions, vous étiez, ils étaient

Study these test sentences for practice. You should aim to be able to translate out of and into French with either column covered.

J'étais arrivé juste à temps.	I had arrived in the nick of time.
L'autobus était parti dix minutes plus tôt.	The bus had gone ten minutes earlier.
Nous avions visité la Tour Eiffel l'été précédent.	We had visited the Eiffel Tower the previous summer.
Vous étiez sortis de la maison avant son arrivée.	You had left the house before he arrived.
Ils étaient partis sans dire au revoir.	They had left without saying goodbye.

Translate into English 1 Nous étions rentrés de bonne heure. 2 J'avais choisi une robe bleue. 3 Il avait déjà vu le film. 4 Elles étaient arrivées avant moi. 5 Tu avais oublié ton parapluie?

Recognition of the past historic

1 You need only to recognize this tense in translations or comprehensions.
2 It is a tense sometimes used instead of the perfect:
   il arriva   he arrived   ils partirent   they left
3 You will only see it in the il/elle or ils/elles form.
4 The endings to look out for are:
   il/elle   *-a -it -ut*
   ils/elles *-èrent -irent -urent*
5 Check from the verb tables as to how the past historic stem of the regular and irregular verbs is formed, to which the endings above are added. Note *venir* and *tenir* especially.

Translate into English 1 Elle partit à minuit. **2** Ils travaillèrent toute la journée. **3** Il but son café. **4** Ils allèrent au café. **5** 'Bonjour,' me dit-il. **6** Elle vint le voir ce soir-là. **7** Ils prirent cette décision. **8** Il plut cette nuit-là. **9** Ils moururent après la bataille. **10** Il fallut partir sans plus tarder. **11** Il mangea une tranche de pain. **12** Ils durent démolir la maison. **13** Elle lui écrivit une lettre. **14** Ils eurent peur tout d'un coup. **15** Elle put s'échapper.

The future tense

1 You will not need to use the future tense much in your written papers and oral test. When you are talking, it is more natural to use *aller* + *infinitive* to say what you are going to do in the near future:
   Je *vais passer* chez ma petite amie ce soir.
   I'm *going to call* at my girlfriend's tonight.
2 You must be able to recognize and understand the future in all parts of your examination.
3 The endings for the future tense are

   je *-ai*   nous *-ons*
   tu *-as*   vous *-ez*
   il *-a*   ils *-ont*

4 Add these endings to the infinitive for regular *-er* and *-ir* verbs:

   donn*er* (to give)   je donner*ai* I will give
                        ils donner*ont* they will give
   fin*ir* (to finish) vous finir*ez* you will finish
                        nous finir*ons* we will finish

5 Add the same endings to the infinitive minus the -e for regular -re verbs:

vend*re* (to sell)   je vend*rai*   I will sell
attend*re* (to wait)   ils attend*ront*   they will wait

6 Learn any irregular verb patterns from the future column in the irregular verb tables. The *endings* always remain the same even where the future stem differs from the infinitive:

av*oir* (to have)   j'aur*ai*   I will have
pouv*oir* (to be able) il pour*ra*   he will be able
all*er* (to go)   ils ir*ont*   they will go

Translate into English 1 Il faudra partir tout de suite. 2 Il m'enverra une carte postale. 3 Ils viendront vers six heures. 4 Tu pourras m'accompagner. 5 Elle voudra faire sa toilette avant de dîner. 6 Vous devrez vous mettre en route très tôt. 7 J'y irai tout seul. 8 Elle sera contente de me voir. 9 Nous aurons beaucoup à faire demain matin. 10 Qu'est-ce que tu feras après les grandes vacances?

Translate into French 11 I will be sixteen in June. 12 I will be sad to leave school. 13 I will be able to go to France next year. 14 We shall be in Paris in eight days. 15 My brother will go to Paris next year.

The conditional tense
1 You will not need to use the conditional much in your written tests, but you may well need to use it in your oral. You must be able to recognize and understand it in all tests.
2 The conditional is used to express what you *would* do in certain circumstances at some *future* time. (However, remember to use the *imperfect* tense in sentences where you are saying/describing what you used to do in the *past*; e.g. 'Every day I would get up late, swallow my coffee and I would almost miss my bus.' 'Chaque jour je me levais tard, j'avalais mon café et je ratais presque mon autobus.')
Examples of use of conditional tense:
I said I *would* call tomorrow.
  J'ai dit que je passer*ais* demain.

If I were to win the pools, I *would* buy a yacht.

Si je gagnais aux pronostics de football, j'achèter*ais* un yacht.

3 In French the conditional uses the same stem as the future tense, but the endings are:

je *-ais*   nous *-ions*
tu *-ais*   vous *-iez*
il *-ait*   ils   *-aient*

Je viendr*ais* si j'avais le temps.

  I *would* come if I had the time.

Papa achèter*ait* une Rolls s'il gagnait aux pronostics de football.

  Dad *would* buy a Rolls if he won the pools

Translate into English 1 Maman a dit qu'elle reviendrait avant six heures.   **2** Il ferait fortune s'il allait aux États-Unis.   **3** Je serais content de la revoir.   **4** Je ne saurais pas quoi faire.   **5** J'irais en Suisse, si j'avais assez d'argent.   **6** Si j'étais à votre place, je ne boirais pas ce cinquième verre de vin rouge.   **7** Ils avaient expliqué qu'ils arriveraient un peu en retard.   **8** Je lui ai dit que je lui enverrais une lettre.   **9** J'aurais peur si j'y allais tout seul.   **10** Il nous a dit qu'il nous verrait le lendemain.

Translate into French 11 If I were rich (Si j'étais riche) . . . I would go on a cruise.   **12** . . . I would take breakfast in bed.   **13** . . . I would go to Canada.   **14** . . . I would drink champagne.   **15** . . . I would drive a Rolls.   **16** . . . I would no longer work.   **17** . . . I would offer 50 franc tips.   **18** . . . I would travel by Concorde.   **19** . . . I would eat in chic restaurants.   **20** . . . I would be happier, perhaps!

The present tense

1 Don't forget to revise the present tense forms of the regular and vital irregular verbs in the verb tables.
2 You will need to use the present tense if there is dialogue in this tense in the English to French translation paper and you will certainly need to use the present in the oral test. You may well be asked what you do in certain situations or to describe what someone else is doing on a picture.
3 The present tense *je travaille* in French can be translated as *I work*, *I am working* or *I do work*, whichever sounds most natural in English.

Translate into French 1 They're putting the cases in the car.
2 We drink tea at breakfast. **3** You have to leave straightaway, my friends. **4** Yes, I do know Paris well. **5** Do you take sugar, sir? **6** She's coming tomorrow. **7** I'm reading a detective novel. **8** The train departs at eight o'clock. **9** They're making a fortune. **10** We write a lot in French. **11** I'm going out tonight. **12** I can see you tomorrow. **13** My mother drives me to school. **14** I know that I'm right. **15** They're going to the match on Saturday.

How well do you know all your tenses?

1 You will have realized by now how important it is to know the tenses of the common verbs for the different parts of your examination.

2 Each of the preceding sections on the different tenses explains one point at a time and then tests you on that point. Things will not be as neat and clear-cut as this in the examination. You will have to cope with many different tenses all on the same paper, either in a written or spoken form.

3 The tests on this page 'jumble up' all the material you should know. By the end of the year you should not be making many mistakes if you have been revising your verbs regularly!

Translate into English 1 Je boirais encore un verre, si je ne prenais pas le volant. **2** Ils couraient vers la sortie. **3** Je lis le journal. **4** Nous ferons du ski dans les Alpes. **5** Tu viens? **6** Il m'avait vu la semaine précédente. **7** Il a sorti son bic. **8** Les enfants mettent les provisions dans le panier. **9** Je voudrais aller en Chine. **10** Il sortait de la maison quand la police est arrivée. **11** Les soldats vinrent à son secours. **12** Il fut étonné. **13** Il tenait un revolver à la main. **14** Elle est devenue célèbre. **15** Les deux femmes finirent leur repas et quittèrent la salle.

Translate into French 16 The family arrived in France. **17** I was opening the door when the telephone rang. **18** I drink a cup of coffee at eight in the morning. **19** He was wearing a green jacket. **20** He read the letter and wrote a reply. **21** They say they are rich. **22** I'm going to make the beds. **23** He gave a tip to the employee. **24** I am doing my homework. **25** She got up at six o'clock. **26** He put the books on the table. **27** It was raining and the sky was black. **28** She will be pleased. **29** They drove to the station. **30** They were going to the station when they saw the thief.

Important verbs

Devoir (to have to, to be obliged to)

1 The verb following devoir must be in the infinitive.

Je *dois travailler* jusqu'à six heures. I have to work until six.

2 The four most common usages are:

present tense   nous *devons observer* le règlement
         we must observe the rules

imperfect   je *devais rentrer* à dix heures quand j'avais quatorze ans
         I used to have to be in at ten when I was fourteen
         years old
         il *devait terminer* son travail ce soir-là
         he was to finish his work that evening

perfect   il *a dû quitter* la maison
         he had to leave the house (i.e. on a particular
         occasion) or he must have left the house

conditional   vous *devriez travailler* dur
         you ought to work hard

Translate into English 1 Je devais aller à l'école à pied quand nous n'avions pas de voiture. **2** Ils devraient respecter leurs parents. **3** On n'a trouvé aucune trace de lui – il a dû s'échapper. **4** Je dois vous quitter maintenant. **5** J'ai dû rentrer tout de suite.

Pouvoir (to be able)

1 The verb following pouvoir must be in the infinitive:

Je *peux venir* demain. I can, am able to, come tomorrow.

2 The four most common usages are:

present tense   je *peux rentrer* à n'importe quelle heure
         I can come home at any time of the day or night

imperfect   il *pouvait aller* à pied à l'école
         he was able to (could) go to school on foot

perfect   ils *ont pu se sauver*
         they managed to run away

conditional   cela *pourrait être* vrai
         that might be true

Translate into English 1 Quand j'avais vingt-cinq ans, je pouvais me coucher tard et me lever tôt. 2 Vous pouvez entrer dans le bureau de M. le Directeur, maintenant. 3 Il pourrait arriver demain. 4 Je n'ai pas pu réparer la voiture. 5 Pourriez-vous faire ce type de travail?

Vouloir (to wish, to want)

1 The verb following vouloir must be in the infinitive.

Je *voudrais parler* à M. le Directeur Général.

I would like to speak to the Managing Director.

2 The four most common usages are:

present tense in question form   *Voulez-vous* bien *fermer* la porte?
                                  Would you mind closing the door?

conditional   je *voudrais vous voir* immédiatement
               I would like to see you straightaway

imperfect   il *voulait* toujours *devenir* médecin
               he always wanted to become a doctor

perfect   ils *ont voulu quitter* l'hôtel ce soir même
               they wanted to leave (insisted on leaving) the hotel
               that very evening

Translate into English 1 Voulez-vous bien me passer le sel? 2 Quand il a vu sa femme, M. Legrand a voulu faire venir le médecin tout de suite. 3 Après de longues journées de travail elle voulait se coucher tôt. 4 Ils voudraient faire une croisière. 5 Veux-tu bien ranger tes affaires?

Avoir (to have)

Learn carefully the following expressions which use avoir in French, often where we use the verb to be in English:

avoir chaud	to feel hot (of a person)
avoir faim	to feel hungry
avoir raison	to be right
avoir seize ans	to be sixteen years old
avoir peur de	to be frightened of
avoir froid	to feel cold (of a person)
avoir soif	to feel thirsty
avoir tort	to be wrong
avoir besoin de	to need
avoir mal à	to have a pain in

Translate into French 1 They are right. 2 You're wrong, gentlemen. 3 His foot was hurting. 4 She was eighteen years old. 5 Are you thirsty? 6 They felt hungry. 7 I need money. 8 She felt hot. 9 Are you cold? 10 Paul was frightened of his teacher.

Faire (to do, to make)
Learn carefully the following expressions which use faire:

faire les achats	to do the shopping
faire la cuisine	to do the cooking
faire le ménage	to do the housework
faire la vaisselle	to do the washing-up
faire une excursion	to go on an outing, trip
faire une promenade	to go for a walk
faire un séjour	to stay
faire du camping	to go camping

Translate into French 1 Mrs Cottard used to do the shopping at the supermarket. 2 He was doing the washing-up when his wife arrived. 3 I stayed in France for three weeks. (say, 'I made a stay of three weeks in France.') 4 We're going to go for a walk this afternoon. 5 Dad does the housework at our house. 6 We were staying in Germany when the accident happened. 7 They went on an outing by car. 8 I do the cooking when we go camping. 9 Shall we go for a walk? 10 Mark and Sandra were going to do the washing-up but they were too tired.

Verbs which can be followed by an infinitive

1 We have already noted that *vouloir*, *pouvoir* and *devoir* can be followed by a second verb in the infinitive:
   il *voudrait partir* he would like to leave
2 In this next section you will learn some more verbs which can be followed by a second verb in the infinitive. Study each of the following four types of construction, making sure you understand the differences in the ways in which the sentences are written.

A Aller, entendre, voir, aimer, préférer

Nous *allons partir*.
  We are going to leave.
J'*entends* le bébé *pleurer*.
  I (can) hear the baby crying.
J'*ai vu* mon père *travailler* dans le jardin.
  I saw my father working in the garden.
Il *aime jouer* au tennis.
  He likes playing tennis.
Elle *préfère sortir* seule.
  She prefers going out on her own.

Translate into French 1 They saw the thief leaving the shop.
2 I heard the burglar going into the lounge.   **3** It was going to rain.
4 Do you like watching telly?   **5** We used to prefer dining at home.

B Aider à, commencer à, continuer à, réussir à, passer (heures) à

J'*ai aidé* maman *à faire* la vaisselle.
  I helped mum do the washing-up.
Il *a commencé à pleurer*.
  He began to weep.
Nous *avons continué à parler* et *à rire*.
  We went on talking and laughing.
L'homme *a réussi à sauver* le garçon.
  The man succeeded in saving the boy.
L'élève *passait* deux heures *à faire* ses devoirs.
  The pupil used to spend two hours doing his homework.

Translate into French 1 I spend two hours each evening listening
to my transistor.   **2** It began to rain.   **3** The policeman succeeded in
arresting (to arrest = arrêter) the criminal.   **4** He went on reading his
book.   **5** I was helping Dad to clean the car when he arrived.

C Décider de, essayer de, cesser de, refuser de, oublier de

Nous *avons décidé de partir*.
  We decided to leave.
Ils *ont essayé d'ouvrir* la porte.
  They tried to open the door.
Il *a cessé de pleuvoir*.
  It stopped raining.

Elle *a refusé de voir* son ami.
  She refused to see her boyfriend.
J'*ai oublié d'apporter* mon imper.
  I've forgotten to bring my mac.

Translate into French **1** It stopped snowing. **2** They decided to
eat at the restaurant. **3** He used to try to speak German. **4** The man
refused to leave. **5** He had forgotten to do his homework.

**D Demander à ... de, dire à ... de, défendre à ... de, permettre
   à ... de**
Le professeur *a demandé aux* élèves *de quitter* la salle.
  The teacher asked the pupils to leave the room.
La mère *a dit au* jeune garçon *de mettre* ses gants.
  The mother told the young boy to put his gloves on.
Le capitaine *a défendu aux* soldats *de parler*.
  The captain did not allow the soldiers to talk.
Il *permet à* son fils *de fumer*.
  He allows his son to smoke.

Translate into English **1** Il nous avait dit de stationner la voiture
devant l'immeuble. **2** Le fermier leur a défendu de pénétrer dans le
champ. **3** Le père ne permettait pas à sa fille de rentrer tard.
4 J'ai demandé à l'agent de nous aider. **5** On lui avait dit d'apporter
un parapluie.

Articles

Many students are confused about when to put *le, la, l', les* in front of a
noun and when to put *du, de la, de l', des*. You will, however, have to
decide because normally a noun cannot stand on its own.

1 Use *le, la, l', les* in the following two types of sentences:
   J'adore *les* frites.
     I love chips (all chips, chips in general).
   Je déteste *les* profs.
     I hate teachers (all teachers, teachers in general).
   C'est *le* cahier dont j'ai besoin pour le prochain cours.
     It's the book I need for the next lesson (same usage as English 'the').

2 Use *du, de la, de l', des* in sentences where you can fit in the word *some* or *any* in the English translation:

Je vais manger *des* frites ce soir.
  I'm having (*some*) chips tonight.
J'ai *des* amis là-bas.
  I've got (*some*) friends over there.
Tu vas m'acheter *du* chocolat?
  Are you going to buy me *some* chocolate?
Vous avez *du* lait?
  Do you have *any* milk?

Translate into French 1 I saw the two men inside the café. **2** There were women in the car. **3** I like biscuits. **4** I usually have cheese instead of a dessert. **5** Do you have any red wine? **6** There are flies in my soup. **7** Do you want chips or potatoes? **8** I hate books.

Negatives

1 You need to know the following negatives:

(a) ne . . . pas   not
(b) ne . . . plus   no more, no longer
(c) ne . . . jamais   never
(d) ne . . . rien   nothing
(e) ne . . . personne   nobody
(f) ne . . . que   only

2 Word order for (a) (b) (c) and (d) – the finite verb is sandwiched between *ne* and the *second negative word*:

Je *n*'ai *pas* fini mon travail.
  I have not finished my work.
Tu *ne* finiras *pas* avant six heures.
  You will not finish before six o'clock.
Il *ne* fume *plus*.
  He no longer smokes.
Elle *n*'est *jamais* allée en France.
  She has never been to France.

Note the pattern for reflexive verbs though:

Il *ne s'*est *pas* dépêché.
  He did not hurry.
Je *ne me* suis *pas* peigné.
  I haven't combed my hair.

3 Word order for (e) and (f) is the same except in the perfect tense, when the second negative word *personne* and *que* comes after the past participle:

Je *n'*ai vu *personne*.
  I saw nobody.
Tu *n'*as mangé *que* six bonbons.
  You have only eaten six sweets.

4 Note how *nobody* is written when it starts the sentence:

personne ne fume	nobody smokes
personne n'était là	nobody was there
personne n'a vu le crime	nobody saw the crime

Translate into French 1 She ate nothing. **2** I don't smoke.
3 We didn't hurry. **4** The policeman saw nobody. **5** He doesn't drink any more. **6** Nobody was talking. **7** He only drank one litre of beer.

No . . . not any

When speaking or writing a sentence in the negative you may want to say *not any, no more, no*, e.g. 'We don't have any money,' 'I've no more beer,' 'We've no television.' In French *any* after a negative is *de* or *d'*:

Nous *n'*avons *pas d'*argent.
  We don't have any money.
Je *n'*ai *plus de* bière.
  I've no more beer.
Il *n'*y a *pas de* supermarché dans le quartier.
  There is no supermarket in the district.
Il *n'*a *plus d'*encre.
  There is no more ink.

Translate into French 1 I've no friends. **2** There's no shower.
3 I'm full up (say 'I've no more appetite'.) **4** They've no more glasses in the pub. **5** There isn't any room (say 'place'). **6** I've no chocolate.

Interrogatives

1 Question words are vital. Understanding and answering questions is what the examination is all about.
2 Knowing how to ask questions is vital when writing letters or when speaking French.
3 Study these test sentences for practice. You should aim to be able to translate out of and into French with either column covered.

Qui est-ce qui a mangé ma tablette de chocolat?	Who's eaten my block of chocolate?
Qui est-ce que tu as sorti hier soir?	Whom did you take out last night?
Qu'est-ce que tu as vu à la télévision hier soir?	What did you see on the television last night?
Quand est-ce que tu as fini ton travail?	When did you finish your work?
Où est-ce que tu habites?	Where do you live?
Combien de frères as-tu?	How many brothers have you got?
Pourquoi est-ce qu'il a volé la planche à roulettes?	Why did he steal the skateboard?
Comment est-ce que tu as passé le week-end?	How did you spend the weekend?
Comment est votre maison?	What's your house like?
Quel livre est-ce que vous avez choisi?	Which book have you chosen?
A quelle heure est-ce que l'accident est arrivé?	At what time did the accident happen?
Depuis quand est-ce que tu apprends le français?	How long have you been learning French?
De quoi est-ce qu'ils parlent?	What are they talking about?

Writing questions in your essay

Note this important rule when using the question forms above. After direct speech, the verb of *saying*, *telling* or *asking* comes before its subject.

Study these pairs of examples:

1 Paul a dit, 'Bonjour.'	'Bonjour,' a dit Paul.
2 Ils ont répondu, 'Non, merci.'	'Non, merci,' ont-ils répondu.
3 Elle a demandé, 'Où est-il?'	'Où est-il?' a-t-elle demandé.
4 Les agents ont crié, 'Halte!'	'Halte!' ont crié les agents.

Translate into French 1 'What's your car like?' Nicole asked.
2 He said, 'Goodbye'. **3** 'Hullo,' he said. **4** 'Why?' asked the
policeman. **5** 'Help!' the children shouted.

Adjectives

1 Adjectives must agree in gender and number with the noun to which
  they refer:

  ce garçon est intelligent   ces garçons sont intelligents
  cette jeune fille est intelligente   ces jeunes filles sont intelligentes

2 Adjectives which already end in -e in the masculine spelling behave as
  follows:

  un livre rouge   une voiture rouge
  des livres rouges   des voitures rouges

3 When checking the spelling in your essay or written paper, remember
  the following patterns for adjectives ending in the letters shown:

	masc. sing.	masc. plural	fem. sing.	fem. plural
-el	officiel	officiels	officielle	officielles
-al	national	nationaux	nationale	nationales
-er	premier	premiers	première	premières
-f	neuf	neufs	neuve	neuves
-x	heureux	heureux	heureuse	heureuses

4 The following two adjectives are irregular. Collect examples of others
  from your reading, starting perhaps with *beau, nouveau* and *vieux*:

masc. sing.	masc. plural	fem. sing.	fem. plural
blanc	blancs	blanche	blanches
favori	favoris	favorite	favorites

Fill in the gap in the second of each pair of phrases, using the same
adjective as in the first phrase, but with the correct ending for the
second noun:

1 un homme heureux; des femmes — **2** un cadeau cher; une voiture — **3** un vélo neuf; des voitures — **4** un ton naturel; une réaction — **5** mon livre favori; ma vedette —

Position of adjectives
1 Most adjectives come after the noun in French: *le drapeau français*; *une chemise verte*, but some really common ones come in front:

bon (fem. bonne)	good	mauvais	bad
grand	big, tall	petit	small
joli	pretty	long (fem. longue)	long

2 Some adjectives have a different meaning according to whether they come before or after the noun.

Study these pairs of examples:

ancien	un *ancien* soldat	an 'old' (former, ex-) soldier
	un bâtiment *ancien*	an old (ancient) building
brave	un *brave* garçon	a good lad
	un garçon *brave*	a brave lad
cher	un *cher* ami	a dear friend
	un cadeau *cher*	an expensive present
pauvre	le *pauvre* prof!	poor (old) teacher!
	un prof *pauvre*	a poor (hard-up) teacher
propre	mon *propre* stylo	my own pen
	une chambre *propre*	a clean room

Translate into English 1 C'est un de mes anciens élèves. **2** C'est un cher collègue. **3** C'est ma propre chambre. **4** Tu as une chemise propre? **5** C'est une école très ancienne. **6** C'est un brave homme. **7** C'est une montre chère? **8** C'est un agent de police très brave. **9** La pauvre dame! **10** C'est une dame très pauvre.

Comparisons
Note how comparisons are made using adjectives:

(a) Sylvie est *plus intelligente que* Jean-Paul.
   Sylvie is cleverer than Jean-Paul.
(b) Je suis *moins riche que* mon voisin.
   I am less rich than my neighbour.
(c) Tu es *aussi fatigué que* moi.
   You are as tired as me.

Bon and *mauvais* follow a different pattern in sentences like (a) above:

Ce café est *meilleur que* l'autre.
  This coffee is better than the other.
Cette faute est *pire que* l'autre.
  This mistake is worse than the other.

Translate into English 1 Cela est moins cher. 2 Il est aussi
ambitieux que son père. 3 Je trouve que ce vin est mauvais; celui-là
est meilleur. 4 Le film qu'on a vu à la télé était pire. 5 Elle est plus
belle que sa mère.

Superlatives
Note how superlatives are expressed using adjectives:

C'est le garçon *le plus intelligent* de la classe.
  He's the most intelligent boy in the class.
C'est la jeune fille *la plus intelligente* de la classe.
  She's the most intelligent girl in the class.
C'est l'homme *le moins doué* du groupe.
  He's the least gifted man in the group.
C'est la famille *la moins riche* de l'immeuble.
  It's the least rich family in the block of flats.
Michel est *le meilleur étudiant* de l'école.
  Michel is the best student in the school.
Elle a *la pire mémoire* de la classe.
  She has the worst memory in the class.

Translate into English 1 C'est le plus grand hôtel de Paris. 2 La
Tour Desfautes est le pire hôtel de l'Angleterre. 3 C'est le meilleur
restaurant de la France. 4 J'habite le plus grand immeuble de la ville.
5 C'est la personne la plus intelligente de notre famille. 6 C'est le
monument le moins visité de la région.

Adverbs

1 You will often recognize an adverb in French because of the ending
   -ment, which is very common:
   il a travaillé rapide*ment*   he worked quickly
   c'est absolu*ment* ridicule   it's absolutely ridiculous

2 However, many common adverbs do not end in -*ment*. Can you translate all the following? (Check your answers against the list at the foot of this page.) *Souvent*; *ensuite*; *puis*; *enfin*; *vite*; *toujours*; *tôt*; *tard*; *assez*; *trop*; *loin*; *tout près*; *demain*; *hier*; *tout de suite*.

3 Note especially:

il travaille *bien* he works well   elle lit *mal* she reads badly
il travaille *mieux* he works better   elle lit *pis* she reads worse

Translate into English 1 Cela se passe rarement. 2 Ils mangent souvent au restaurant. 3 Tu as vite fini! 4 Tu es rentré tard hier soir. 5 Il écrit mieux en français que sa sœur. 6 Il joue bien. 7 Tu lis mal. 8 Tant pis! 9 Tant mieux! 10 Décrivez exactement ce que vous avez vu. 11 Evidemment vous avez raison. 12 Il est assez intelligent.

Expressions of quantity

Expressions of quantity *a lot of*, *a kilo of*, *a litre of* are followed by *de* or *d'* in French.

Study the test sentences for practice. You should aim to be able to translate out of and into French, with either column covered.

beaucoup de gens	a lot of people
trop de fautes	too many mistakes
assez d'argent	enough money
un peu de discipline	a little discipline
un kilo de bananes	a kilo of bananas
cent grammes de chocolat	100 grammes of chocolate
une bouteille de vin	a bottle of wine
un demi-litre d'eau minérale	half a litre of mineral water
un verre d'eau	a glass of water
un paquet de cigarettes	a packet of cigarettes

Answers Often, then, next, at last, quickly, always, early, late, enough, too much, far, nearby, tomorrow, yesterday, straightaway.

Translate into French 1 too much beer 2 enough intelligence
3 two kilos of apples 4 250 grammes of sweets 5 a bottle of water
6 a packet of tea 7 a little money 8 a lot of friends 9 a glass of
red wine 10 two litres of milk.

Prepositions

A, au, à la, à l', aux

Learn the following phrases:

Rouen est *à* 123 km de Paris.	Rouen is 123 km *from* Paris.
Le train roule *à* 140 km à l'heure.	The train goes *at* 140 km an hour.
Québec se trouve *au* Canada (masculine countries).	Quebec is *in* Canada.
La Tour Eiffel se trouve *à* Paris (towns).	The Eiffel Tower is *in* Paris.
à la campagne; *à la* montagne	in the countryside; in the mountains
au bord de la mer; *au* premier étage	*at* the seaside; *on* the first floor
à pied; *à* cheval	*on* foot; *on* horseback
à midi; *à* trois heures; *à* l'heure	*at* midday; *at* three o'clock; *on* time.
jouer *au* football; jouer *au* hockey	to play football; to play hockey
Je pense *à* ma mère.	I'm thinking *about* my mother.
Il a pris un bonbon *à* sa sœur.	He took a sweet *from* his sister.
Ils ont volé un portefeuille *au* vieux monsieur.	They stole a wallet *from* the old gentleman.

Translate into French 1 The car was ten km from the village. 2 At
sixty k.p.h. 3 He plays tennis. 4 I was thinking about my uncle.
5 On the eleventh floor. 6 In the USA. 7 In London. 8 The
teacher took the exercise book from the pupil.

En

Learn the following phrases:

en France; *en* Belgique (feminine countries)	*in* France; *in* Belgium

une règle *en* bois; un dossier *en* plastique	a wooden ruler; a plastic folder
en avion; *en* autobus; *en* car	*by* plane; *by* bus; *by* coach
en voiture; *en* taxi; *en* vélo	*by* car; *by* taxi; *by* bike
en automne; *en* hiver; *en* été	*in* autumn; *in* winter; *in* summer
en 1979; *en* cinq minutes	*in* 1979; *within* five minutes

Pour

Learn the following phrases:

Le train *pour* Paris.	The train (going) *to* Paris.
Il est assez âgé *pour* fumer.	He's old enough *to* smoke.
Il est trop jeune *pour* se marier.	He's too young *to* get married.
Je vais en France *pour* trois semaines.	I'm going to France *for* three weeks (future time).
Note Je suis resté en France *pendant* trois semaines.	I stayed in France *for* three weeks (past time).

Translate into English 1 C'est bien le train pour Lyon? **2** Un avion en papier. **3** J'ai parlé à mon professeur pendant vingt minutes. **4** Je vais au Canada pour trois semaines. **5** Il est assez intelligent pour réussir à son examen. **6** Il est trop malade pour voyager.

Prepositions of position

You should be able to translate the following words into and out of French, with either column covered.

sur	on
sous	under
dans	in
devant	in front of
derrière	behind
entre	between
contre	against
près de	near to
loin de	far from
en face de	opposite
à côté de	next to
à droite de	on the right of
à gauche de	on the left of
au-dessus de	above
au-dessous de	beneath

Translate into French **1** opposite the post office   **2** above the town
3 on the table   **4** against the wall   **5** between the forest and the lake
6 in front of the supermarket   **7** on the right of the dining room
8 on the left of the cinema   **9** next to the baker's   **10** in the suitcase
11 far from the town   **12** near to the station   **13** behind the house
14 under the chair   **15** next to the swimming pool and the campsite.

Prepositions linking verbs to their objects

Study carefully the pairs of sentences, noting how the two languages are
different in their usages. You should aim to be able to translate out of
and into French, with either column covered.

Il a téléphoné à son père.	He phoned his father.
Elle a donné une récompense au garçon.	She gave the boy a reward.
Le professeur a demandé le cahier à l'élève.	The teacher asked the pupil for the book.
Le garçon a pris un feutre à sa sœur.	The boy took a felt-tip from his sister.
L'agent a montré le panneau à l'automobiliste.	The policeman showed the motorist the sign.
Le marchand a vendu la pomme à la cliente.	The shopkeeper sold the customer the apple.
Ils attendaient le train.	They were waiting for the train.
J'habite Londres.	I live in London.
Je cherche un poste.	I'm looking for a job.
J'ai payé le repas.	I paid for the meal.
Nous regardions sa nouvelle voiture.	We were looking at his new car.
Il écoute la radio.	He's listening to the radio.

Translate into French **1** We looked for the thief.   **2** He used to
live in Madrid.   **3** I waited for a bus.   **4** The policemen took the gun
from the thief.   **5** She showed the lady the bananas.   **6** He was
listening to the music.   **7** The policeman looked at the car.   **8** She
gave the teacher the answer.   **9** He sold his bike to a friend.   **10** They
phoned the police.

Pronouns

1 Pronouns help you to speak and write naturally in French. Study the
pairs of sentences, concentrating especially on the position of the
pronoun, normally immediately before the finite verb.

il *me* donne son cahier	he gives me his book
je ne *te* comprends pas	I don't understand you
je *le* vois; je *la* vois	I see him/it (masc.); I see her/it (fem.)
il *nous* a envoyé un cadeau	He sent us a present
je *vous* ai vu hier soir	I saw you last night
je *les* aime beaucoup	I like them a lot

2 *Me, te, le, la* shorten to *m', t', l'* before a vowel *a, e, i, o, u, y*:

je *l'*ai vu hier soir   I saw him last night

3 *Lui* (to him/to her) *leur* (to them)
Use these pronouns with verbs that take *à* before a person.

je *lui* offre un cadeau	I offer him a present
tu *lui* as téléphoné	you telephoned her
je *leur* ai montré mon nouveau vélo	I showed them my new bike
il *leur* a parlé	he spoke to them

4 When pronouns are linked to an infinitive in a sentence they normally
come before that infinitive:

je vais *lui parler*	I'm going to speak to him
je voudrais *le voir* demain	I would like to see him tomorrow

5 The pronouns for *me, you, him, her* and *them* have a special form
after *pour, sans, avec*:

pour moi	for me	avec lui	with him	pour eux	for them (masc.)
sans toi	without you	sans elle	without her	sans elles	without them (fem.)

Translate into English 1 Je leur ai demandé la raison.   2 Le
monsieur lui a vendu la voiture.   3 Il m'a vu à la Poste.   4 Je
t'écrirai la semaine prochaine.   5 Je vais vous parler plus tard dans la
journée.   6 Tes livres? Je les ai vus dans le vestibule.   7 Tu
m'écriras, n'est-ce pas?   8 On leur avait permis de sortir.   9 Je lui ai
dit de rentrer tôt, mais elle n'est pas encore revenue.   10 Il m'a
demandé d'éteindre ma pipe.

Translate into French 11 I don't understand them.   12 I rang her up last week.   13 I will speak to him tomorrow.   14 The film? I saw it on telly last night.   15 He asked Alain the time.   16 He talks to us.   17 I would like to see them in my office.   18 I spoke to her last Tuesday.   19 Do you hear me?   20 He showed him his driving licence.

Note Using pronouns in your essay will certainly make it sound more natural, but accuracy is all important in the O level examination, so remember the golden rule: only use what you feel you can confidently and competently handle!

Three final pronouns Y EN, ON

1 *Y* often replaces a noun or place, when it is translated as *there*:

> Vous passez vos vacances à Madrid? Oui, j'*y* vais mardi prochain.
>   Are you spending your holidays in Madrid? Yes, I'm going there
>   next Tuesday.
> Tu es allé à la piscine? J'*y* suis allé hier soir.
>   Have you been to the swimming pool? I went there last night.

2 *En* is used

  (a) to replace *de* + *noun*
    Elle est sortie de l'église? Elle *en* est sortie il y a cinq minutes.
    Has she come out of the church? She came out of it five minutes
    ago.
  (b) with numbers or expressions of quantity, meaning *some, of it, of them*. We would not normally translate *en* by an English word
    Combien de frères as-tu? J'*en* ai trois; je n'*en* ai pas.
    How many brothers have you got? I have three; I don't have any.
    Tu as des cousins? J'*en* ai beaucoup.
    Do you have any cousins? I have a lot.

3 *On* can be translated in different ways: *one* (usually the least satisfactory translation into English) *they, people, someone, we.*

| On parle français au Sénégal. | They speak French in Senegal. |
| On dansait et on chantait. | People were dancing and singing. |

Note this way of translating *on*:

| On a fini le travail à six heures. | The work was finished at six o'clock. |
| On m'a dit de plier bagages. | I was told to pack up and go. |

In speech *on* is nearly always used instead of *nous*:

On a bien mangé, on a bien bu.   We ate well and drank well.
On va voir le film?   Shall we go and see the film?

Translate into English **1** Il y avait vu son père.   **2** Tu as un bic?
J'en ai deux.   **3** Elle n'a pas de cousins. Si! Elle en a un.   **4** Elle y va
mardi prochain.   **5** On va voir.   **6** On va rentrer vers cinq heures.
7 On boit plus de vin en France qu'en Angleterre.   **8** On m'a réveillé
à quatre heures.   **9** On s'est bien amusé, n'est-ce pas?   **10** On lui a
dit de se taire.

Useful constructions for your essay

You will give a good impression by using the following constructions
accurately in your essay, but only use them if you are sure you are not
going to make mistakes. If in doubt, play safe!

1 *venir de* + *infinitive*

  (a) used in the present tense
     je viens de terminer mon travail   I have just finished my work
     tu viens de terminer ton travail   you have just . . .
     il vient de terminer son travail   he has just . . .

  (b) used in the imperfect tense
     je venais de terminer mon travail   I had just finished my work
     tu venais de terminer ton travail   you had just . . .
     il venait de terminer son travail   he had just . . .

2 *Après avoir* + *past participle*
  Après être + *past participle* + *agreement*
  Après s'être + *past participle* + *agreement*
  Après avoir allumé sa cigarette, il a toussé.
    After having lit his cigarette, he coughed.
  Après être arrivée, elle est montée à sa chambre.
    After her arrival, she went upstairs to her bedroom.
  Après m'être rasé, je me suis lavé.
    When I had shaved, I washed myself.
  Après s'être lavée, elle est descendue.
    When she had washed, she went downstairs.

3 *Avant de + infinitive*

Avant de parler, il a consulté ses notes.

Before speaking, he consulted his notes.

4 *Au lieu de + infinitive*

Au lieu de fumer sa pipe, il fumait une cigare.

Instead of smoking his pipe, he was smoking a cigar.

5 *Sans + infinitive*

Sans hésiter, il a commencé son discours.

Without hesitating, he began his speech.

6 *Pour + infinitive*

Pour réussir, il faut travailler.

In order to succeed, you have to work.

7 *Être en train de + infinitive*

Il était en train de prendre son petit déjeuner quand le téléphone a sonné.

He *was in the middle of having* his breakfast when the phone went.

8 *Être sur le point de + infinitive*

J'étais sur le point d'accepter une offre que je ne pouvais pas réfuser.

I *was on the point of accepting* an offer I couldn't refuse.

9 *Depuis*

(a) used with the present tense

J'attends *depuis* six heures.

I*'ve been* waiting *for* six hours.

Il travaille ici *depuis* deux ans.

He*'s been* working here *for* two years.

(b) used with the imperfect tense

J'attend*ais depuis* six heures.

I *had been* waiting *for* six hours.

Il travaill*ait* ici *depuis* deux ans.

He *had been* working here *for* two years.

Translate into French **1** I was in the middle of washing the car when he arrived. **2** We had just arrived. **3** You have been talking for half an hour. **4** She was about to enter the house. **5** Before finishing the work he smoked a cigarette. **6** He worked without talking. **7** We work in order to earn money. **8** I've just arrived. **9** He had been waiting a long time. **10** Having got up to the tenth floor I was tired. **11** When she had finished her work she rested. **12** When she had combed her hair she got dressed.

2   Revising vocabulary

A good vocabulary is an important asset in all parts of the examination. In this section vocabulary has been broken down into themes (*la maison/l'appartement, au-delà de l'école, les animaux* etc) to facilitate learning and revision work. The themes chosen represent those topics which feature most regularly in the examination. You are expected to understand all the words on the left hand pages, so that you should be able to translate from French into English. The words printed in **bold type** (they can be nouns, adjectives, verbs etc) are key words which should be familiar to you. You should be able to translate these words from English into French. Remember, however, that the particular translations offered in this book depend largely on the context in which the key words are used. Remember also that if you do not know or are unsure of the gender of these key words, *check them in your dictionary*.

Finally, although what is given here is the *minimum* requirement – and you should always look to increase your vocabulary – do bear in mind that you will need to understand far more words (whether they are written or heard in French) than you will be required to say or write: recognizing the English meaning of a word is far easier than either having to say it or write it in French.

Suggested method of working

Each double page spread is designed as a unit on a theme, e.g. *l'identité*; *les passe-temps*; *les transports*. Work on one unit at a time (the order does not matter) keeping a record of the work you do in each session. Your vocabulary will greatly improve if you work at a steady rate and do not leave it all to the last minute. If possible, work in quiet conditions, concentrating really hard on the revision work you have set yourself.

Follow the steps below. These do not have to be completed all in one session but remember to record in your notes how far you get.

1 Work on the left-hand page first. Read the English and the French sentences carefully at least three times.

2 Cover up the English sentences, study the French sentences and see how much you can translate into English. Pay particular attention to the words in bold type in French. If you get stuck, uncover the English translation. Keep on working like this until you can translate all the sentences from French into English. For a change, test yourself in writing or ask a friend or relative who can speak French to read out the sentence for you to translate into English.

3 Now cover the French sentences. Read the English sentences and say or write down the French for the words in bold type. Work in the same kind of way as in Step 2, again getting a friend or relative to test you sometimes. Spelling is vital so write down words as well as saying them. Don't forget to learn the gender of nouns.

4 Repeat the whole process with the short word lists at the foot of the left-hand page. These are words which you must know how to translate into and out of French.

5 Cover over the left-hand page and choose one of the tests on the right-hand page to check how well you know the vocabulary theme. The tests are mainly of the following type:

Translation English–French and French–English
Compréhension   A short text is followed by a series of statements. In each case you must choose the statement which is correct, based on the information given in the text.
De quoi est-ce qu'on parle?/De quelle activité est-ce qu'on parle?   Here a word/action is defined for you in French; from this you must work out the French word (it can be a noun or a verb) which best describes the particular action/word.
Complétez la phrase   In this test you are asked to work out the correct French word missing in a given sentence: sometimes you will be asked to choose from several suggested answers, sometimes you will be asked to work out the French word for yourself.
Qu'est-ce qu'on répondrait?   Here you are asked to choose the most likely reply – from several suggested answers – to the remark which is made.
Questions orales   These are typical questions which you may be asked in the oral examination about yourself, your family and the area in which you live. You should answer them out loud.

Sometimes the tests will contain words not given on the left-hand page. You must make an intelligent guess at the meaning of such words, just as you will have to in the actual examination.

1 L'identité

1 **J'ai seize ans,** je suis de taille moyenne (je mesure 1 m 50) et je pèse 70 kilos.

1 **I'm sixteen years old,** of average height (I'm 1 metre 50 tall) and I weigh 70 kilos.

2 Je **suis né(e)** le 15 novembre 1964 à Nancy dans l'est de la France.

2 I **was born** on the 15th November 1964 in Nancy in the east of France.

3 J'ai les **yeux** verts et les **cheveux** roux.

3 My **eyes** are green and I've got red **hair**.

4 Je suis **fils** (**fille**) unique – c'est-à-dire que je n'ai ni **frères** ni **sœurs**.

4 I'm an only **son** (**daughter**) – that's to say I've no **brothers** or **sisters**.

5 Mon **père** est camionneur; il conduit son poids-lourd un peu partout en France.

5 My **father** is a lorry driver; he drives his truck all over France.

6 Ma **mère** est sans profession. Elle est ménagère.

6 My **mother** doesn't have a paid job. She's a housewife.

7 Comme **tout le monde** j'ai fait cinq ans à l'école primaire avant d'aller au CES à l'âge de 11.

7 Like **everybody else** I did five years at primary school before going to the comprehensive at the age of 11.

8 Je suis **élève** du CET depuis un an maintenant.

8 I've been a **pupil** at the technical college for a year now.

9 J'espère devenir apprenti(e) ingénieur en fin de mes études.

9 I hope to become an engineering apprentice at the end of my studies.

10 Je suis un(e) mordu(e) du cinéma – c'est mon **passe-temps** favori.

10 I'm really keen on films – it's my favourite **pastime**.

11 J'ai un emploi à temps partiel. Je **travaille** au **marché** le **samedi**.

11 I have a part-time job. I **work** on the **market** on **Saturdays**.

12 Avec l'**argent** que je gagne je fais des économies pour m'acheter un **vélomoteur**.

12 With the **money** I earn I'm saving up to buy myself a **moped**.

le disque	record	dépenser de	to spend
le lycée	grammar school	l'argent sur . . .	money on . . .
le petit ami	boyfriend	blond	fair (of hair, eyes)
les vêtements	clothes	brun	brown
la petite amie	girlfriend	moins âgé (que)	younger than
se payer	to treat yourself to	plus âgé (que)	older than

A Translate into French
1 She is eighteen.   **2** I was born on the 2nd January 1965.   **3** He had green eyes and black hair.   **4** She's an only daughter.   **5** My brother is a teacher.   **6** My sister goes to a comprehensive school. **7** I've been a pupil of this school for six years.   **8** I'm really keen on sport.

B Translate into English
Mon père est né en 1937, deux ans avant la Deuxième Guerre Mondiale. Après la guerre il est devenu ingénieur et il exerce cette profession depuis plus de trente ans maintenant. Ma mère travaillait à temps partiel jusqu'à récemment, mais maintenant elle est ménagère. C'est un emploi non-salarié qui exige quand même beaucoup d'efforts. Et moi? Je suis née en 1964 dans une petite ville dans l'ouest de la France. Puisque j'ai eu le bonheur d'être née dans une époque d'émancipation féminine, je suis tout à fait décidée à profiter pleinement de ces chances d'égalité.

C Qu'est-ce qu'on répondrait?
1 Il n'a qu'un frère.
  (*a*) *Il est fils unique.*
  (*b*) *C'est extraordinaire.*
  (*c*) *Mais il est plus âgé.*
2 Je suis élève au lycée depuis plus de trois ans maintenant.
  (*a*) *Tu n'es plus étudiant au lycée.*
  (*b*) *C'est ta quatrième année, alors.*
  (*c*) *Tu n'y vas plus depuis ta troisième année.*
3 J'aimerais m'acheter un nouveau vélo, mais ça coûte cher!
  (*a*) *Il faut que tu fasses encore des économies.*
  (*b*) *Il faut que tu ne fasses plus d'économies.*
  (*c*) *Tu devrais acheter un vélomoteur.*

D Questions orales
1 De quelle couleur sont vos cheveux et vos yeux?
2 Combien pesez-vous et combien mesurez-vous?
3 Quand et où êtes-vous né?
4 Est-ce que vous êtes enfant unique?
5 Faites le portrait de quelqu'un que vous connaissez.
6 Est-ce que vous faites des économies? Comment? Est-ce qu'il y a quelque chose de spécial que vous aimeriez-vous acheter?
7 Qu'avez-vous fait de votre argent de poche la semaine dernière?

2 La maison, l'appartement

1 Nous **habitons** un **appartement** qui comprend sept **pièces** au troisième étage d'un immeuble:

1 We **live** in a **flat** with seven **rooms** on the third floor of a block:

2 **salle de séjour, salle à manger, cuisine, salle de bain,** w.c. et trois chambres.

2 **living room, dining room, kitchen, bathroom,** toilet and three bedrooms.

3 La **concierge** de l'immeuble distribue le courrier et **nettoie l'escalier.**

3 The **caretaker** for the block distributes the mail and **cleans the staircase.**

4 Nous **trouvons** le chauffage central pratique en hiver et facile à régler.

4 We **find** the central heating handy in winter and easy to adjust.

5 Nos **meubles** ne sont pas du dernier style, mais ils sont quand même confortables.

5 Our **furniture** isn't in the latest style, but it's comfortable all the same.

6 Ma **mère** est une passionnée de l'électroménager.

6 My **mother** is very keen on domestic appliances.

7 Elle aimerait s'acheter un lave-vaisselle et un congélateur.

7 She'd like to buy herself a dishwasher and a freezer.

8 Le rêve de beaucoup de citadins français est une **maison** individuelle.

8 The dream of lots of French town dwellers is a detached **house.**

9 Devant cette maison il y aurait une pelouse et plusieurs parterres.

9 In front of this house there would be a lawn and several flowerbeds.

10 Qu'est-ce qui gâterait cette image de tranquillité?

10 What would spoil this picture of tranquillity?

11 Ce serait moi qui devrais tondre le gazon!

11 I'm the one who would have to cut the lawn!

12 Je crois que je **préfère** ma petite **chambre** en désordre, où je peux laisser traîner mes affaires un peu partout!

12 I think I **prefer** my tiny, untidy **bedroom** where I can leave my things lying all over the place!

un aspirateur	vacuum cleaner	le réfrigérateur	fridge
le canapé	sofa	le salon	lounge
le fauteuil	armchair	une armoire	wardrobe/cupboard
le grenier	attic	la cave	cellar
le lit	bed	la commode	chest of drawers

A Translate into English

Nous avons la chance d'habiter une maison – à la différence de la plupart des Français qui sont obligés de demeurer dans des grands immeubles. Notre maison est un peu démodée, mais on se sent quand même chez soi. Les pièces sont de dimensions généreuses, avec une grande salle de séjour au rez-de-chaussée. Notre famille est nombreuse et puisque je suis le cadet on m'a accordé une petite chambre au grenier; elle ne mesure que 3 mètres sur 2. Malgré ses dimensions elle me plaît beaucoup, avec son papier peint vert clair. L'ambiance de cette vieille maison nous a apporté beaucoup de joie au cours des années, ce qui prouve que les appareils du 20e siècle – fours micro-onde, chauffage à air pulsé, lave-vaisselle – dont tout le monde semble être obsédé, ne sont pas aussi indispensables que nous laisse supposer la publicité.

B Qu'est-ce qu'on répondrait?

1 On va passer dans la salle de séjour?
  (a) *Oui, j'y suis passé.*
  (b) *Oui, on va manger après le séjour.*
  (c) *D'accord – on va y prendre le café.*

2 Tu as vu ma nouvelle commode?
  (a) *Oui, c'est une commode.*
  (b) *Oui, je vais avoir de tes nouvelles.*
  (c) *Celle dans la petite chambre au grenier?*

3 Qu'est-ce qu'elle est en train de faire, la concierge?
  (a) *Elle va courir.*
  (b) *Elle distribuait des lettres.*
  (c) *Elle s'occupe des lettres.*

4 Regarde ma pelouse après trois semaines d'absence!
  (a) *Il faudra sortir la tondeuse.*
  (b) *Il faudra de la tendresse.*
  (c) *Le gazon est court, n'est-ce pas?*

C Questions orales

1 Où se trouve votre maison ou votre appartement?
2 Décrivez votre chambre.
3 A quoi sert un aspirateur?
4 Comment serait votre maison idéale?
5 Que fait le concierge d'un immeuble français?

---

peint en vert	painted green
mesurer 4 mètres sur 5	to measure 4 metres by 5

3 La routine quotidienne

1 C'est bizarre: je me **réveille** d'habitude cinq minutes avant que sonne mon réveil-matin.

1 It's odd: I usually **wake up** five minutes before my alarm clock goes off.

2 Je **me lève** directement et je **me lave**; j'ai un **lavabo** dans ma **chambre**.

2 I **get up** straightaway and **wash**; I have a **wash-basin** in my **bedroom**.

3 Après m'**être habillé** et peigné, je **descends** pour **prendre mon petit déjeuner**.

3 When I've **dressed** and combed my hair, I **go downstairs** to **have my breakfast**.

4 Ce **matin** j'ai pris du chocolat **chaud** et j'ai mangé mon **pain grillé** habituel.

4 This **morning** I had **hot** drinking chocolate and ate my usual **toast**.

5 Mon **père** était de mauvaise humeur – il s'était coupé à la joue en se rasant.

5 My **father** was in a bad mood – he'd cut his cheek when shaving.

6 Il a avalé quelques gouttes de café et puis il est **sorti en se dépêchant**.

6 He swallowed a few drops of coffee and **rushed out**.

7 Je me suis brossé les **dents** avant de me mettre en route pour le **collège**.

7 I cleaned my **teeth** before setting off for **school**.

8 Le **dimanche** c'est moins frénétique. On fait la grasse matinée et on n'est pas pressé.

8 On **Sundays** it's less hectic. We lie in and we're in less of a hurry.

9 J'**aide** ma **mère** à faire la **vaisselle** et ma sœur l'aide à faire le ménage.

9 I **help** my **mother** do the **washing–up** and my sister helps her to do the housework.

10 Le **dimanche après-midi** on **sort en voiture** ou on fait une **promenade**.

10 On **Sunday afternoons** we **go out in the car** or go for a **walk**.

11 Vers le goûter on se détend devant le **téléviseur** ou on passe un **disque**.

11 Towards tea-time we relax in front of the **television set** or put on a **record**.

12 Le dimanche et les jours fériés on **se couche** plus tard que les jours ouvrables.

12 On Sundays and holidays we **go to bed** later than on working days.

faire les lits	to make the beds	ranger/sortir	put away/get out
laisser tomber	to drop, let slip	ses affaires	your belongings
nettoyer	to clean	renverser	to knock over

A Translate into French

1 Mr Snobinard woke up fifteen minutes before his wife. **2** She got up straightaway and had a wash. **3** I got dressed and combed my hair. **4** They went downstairs to have their breakfast. **5** She was having black coffee and eating bread when the man arrived. **6** They hurried into the room. **7** I used to brush my teeth before going to bed. **8** They set off for church. **9** I was doing the housework and my husband was doing the washing-up. **10** They went out (for a trip) on their bikes. **11** I went for a walk on Tuesday afternoon. **12** The children went to bed very late. **13** She spilt the coffee. **14** He dropped the record.

B De quelle activité est-ce qu'on parle?

1 Action de mettre les cheveux en ordre.
2 Action d'appliquer de la pâte dentifrice sur les dents.
3 Action de mettre ses vêtements.
4 Action d'enlever des poils des joues, du menton.
5 Se presser; agir à la hâte.
6 Laver en eau chaude des assiettes, tasses, soucoupes etc.
7 Nettoyer les meubles et les pièces d'une maison.
8 Marcher tout seul ou en groupe, surtout à la campagne.

C Qu'est-ce qu'on répondrait?

1 Vous n'êtes pas pressé, monsieur?
  (a) *Mais si, je prends un citron pressé.*
  (b) *Mais si, je dois me dépêcher.*
  (c) *Mais oui, je suis frénétique.*
2 On fait la grasse matinée, chérie?
  (a) *Pourquoi pas? C'est un jour férié.*
  (b) *Pourquoi pas? C'est un jour ouvrable.*
  (c) *Pourquoi pas? Tu es déjà si gras ce matin.*
3 J'aime me détendre le weekend.
  (a) *Je m'étends aussi.*
  (b) *Tu m'entends aussi.*
  (c) *Moi aussi – on peut prendre son temps.*

D Questions orales

1 De quoi est-ce qu'on se sert pour faire le ménage?
2 Comment pourriez-vous aider à la maison?
3 Que devez-vous faire avant de vous coucher?
4 Qu'est-ce qu'on fait chez vous le dimanche?
5 Qu'est-ce que vous avez fait ce matin entre sept et neuf heures?

4 La nourriture

1 Le **petit déjeuner** en France est un **repas** léger, moins copieux qu'en Angleterre.

1 **Breakfast** in France is a light **meal**, less hearty than in England.

2 Il consiste d'un **bol de café,** ou de **chocolat chaud,** accompagné de **tartines** beurrées avec de la **confiture.**

2 It consists of a **bowl of coffee,** or **hot chocolate,** accompanied by **slices of bread** and butter with **jam.**

3 Beaucoup de Français ont l'habitude de **manger chez eux** à midi.

3 Lots of French people are in the habit of **eating at home** at **midday.**

4 Comme hors d'œuvre on prendrait peut-être une salade de tomates ou un **œuf** mayonnaise.

4 As a starter they might have tomato salad or **egg** mayonnaise.

5 Comme plat principal, de la **viande** ou du **poisson** garni de **légumes.**

5 As a main dish, **meat** or **fish** served with **vegetables.**

6 Avant le dessert on aurait le choix entre plusieurs fromages sur le plateau.

6 Before the sweet you would have a choice of several types of cheese from the board.

7 Les desserts sont souvent modestes – une **glace,** une **tarte** aux pommes ou un **fruit.**

7 Desserts are often simple – **ice cream,** apple **pie** or **fruit.**

8 C'est du café **noir** qu'**on boit** après un repas. Le café au lait se boit à d'autres moments.

8 **Black** coffee **is taken** after a meal. White coffee is taken at other times.

9 En **été** on prend très **souvent** un panier-repas en plein air.

9 In **summer** a picnic meal is **often** taken in the open air.

10 Quelques tranches de **pain** et du camembert, arrosés de **vin** rouge. **Délicieux** et désaltérant!

10 A few slices of **bread** and some camembert, washed down with **red** wine. **Delicious** and refreshing!

11 Quand maman reçoit, c'est moi qui mets les couverts pour les invités.

11 When mum is entertaining, I'm the one who sets the table for the guests.

12 Au **restaurant** on **commande** ce qu'on veut selon la **carte.**

12 In the **restaurant** you **order** what you want according to the **menu.**

| le garçon/la serveuse | waiter/tress | une addition | bill |
| le menu | fixed price meal | service compris | service included |

A Translate into French

1 He used to have breakfast in the kitchen. 2 He was drinking a
glass of red wine when the girl entered the restaurant. 3 For first
course he chose an egg mayonnaise. 4 They had a light meal – fish
served with vegetables. 5 He ordered a black coffee. 6 The waiter
brought the sweet course. 7 She was entertaining some guests for
dinner.

B Compréhension

J'ai toujours l'impression qu'il y a une foule d'invités chez nous, ce qui
m'embête un peu puisque je suis obligée d'aider maman à faire des
préparatifs. Je dois assurer que tout soit bien en place sur la table et
quelquefois j'aide maman à servir aussi. Il est très agréable d'assister à
un de ces 'banquets' à la fin duquel on n'a plus d'appétit, mais après il
faut faire la vaisselle. On mangerait plus modestement peut-être si on
pensait à cette corvée inévitable.

1 (a) La mère de famille invite des gens fous.
  (b) La mère de famille aime être invitée.
  (c) La mère de famille est un peu embêtée.
  (d) La mère de famille aime recevoir des gens.
2 (a) La jeune fille met les couverts.
  (b) La jeune fille met les couvertures.
  (c) La jeune fille prend une assurance.
  (d) La jeune fille prend sa place à table.
3 (a) A la fin du repas on a plus d'appétit.
  (b) A la fin du repas on ne peut plus rien manger.
  (c) A la fin du repas les invités sont obligés de faire la vaisselle.
  (d) A la fin du repas les invités ont toujours bon appétit.
4 (a) On mangerait plus si on pensait au travail.
  (b) Ceux qui dînent ne pensent pas peut-être au travail qui suit.
  (c) Les invités mangent modestement: c'est inévitable.
  (d) La jeune fille aime faire la vaisselle.

C Questions orales

1 Quelles sont les heures des repas chez vous?
2 Quand est-ce que vous prenez votre repas principal et pourquoi?
3 Quels préparatifs feriez-vous si vous deviez prendre un panier-repas
   en excursion?
4 Quelle est la différence entre 'manger à la carte' et 'prendre le menu'
   dans un restaurant?
5 Préférez-vous manger chez vous ou au restaurant? Pourquoi?

5 Les passe-temps

1 **Tout le monde** a son moyen favori d'occuper ses loisirs.

2 Mon **père vient d'**acheter une chaîne de hi-fi dont il est très fier.

3 Il peut écouter la radio, passer des **disques** ou des cassettes et faire des enregistrements.

4 Je m'**intéresse** à la musique pop plutôt qu'à la musique classique.

5 Les **jeux** intérieurs – échecs, cartes, jeux de société – ne sont pas vraiment de mon goût.

6 Je prends beaucoup de plaisir à faire des **photos** avec mon **appareil** de poche.

7 Ma **mère** est enragée de la lecture – romans historiques, science-fiction, biographies.

8 Mon frère aime emmener sa petite amie au bal le samedi soir.

9 J'ai un **oncle** qui passe ses heures de liberté à faire du bricolage.

10 Il se débrouille bien : il a décoré son **salon** et a peint l'extérieur de sa **maison**.

11 Ma **sœur joue** du violon et du piano avec beaucoup d'adresse.

12 J'ai des copains qui collectionnent des objets bizarres ! A chacun son goût !

1 **Everyone** has his favourite way of filling up his leisure time.

2 My **father has just** bought a music centre of which he's very proud.

3 He can listen to the radio, play **records** or cassettes and make recordings.

4 I'm **interested** in pop music rather than classical music.

5 **Indoor** games – chess, cards, parlour games – aren't really my cup of tea.

6 I get a lot of pleasure from taking **photos** with my pocket **camera**.

7 My **mother** is mad keen on reading – historical novels, science fiction and biographies.

8 My brother likes taking his girlfriend to the dance on Saturday nights.

9 I've an **uncle** who spends his free time on DIY jobs.

10 He manages quite well : he's decorated his **lounge** and painted the outside of his **house**.

11 My **sister plays** the violin and the piano very skilfully.

12 I have friends who collect weird objects ! Everyone to his own taste !

A Translate into English

Tout le monde occupe ses heures de liberté d'une manière qui lui plaît, mais quelquefois on trouve des gens qui ont des goûts bizarres. Mon beau-frère, par exemple, n'est jamais plus content que quand il fait du bricolage, malgré son manque d'adresse. Ma sœur m'a raconté un incident où son mari a essayé de réparer une fuite d'eau dans un radiateur. La petite fuite est devenue une fuite grave et on a fini par faire venir le plombier! Mais en fin de compte ce manque d'adresse n'importe pas. Ce qui est plus important, c'est le plaisir et la détente après une longue journée de travail.

B Qu'est-ce qu'on répondrait?

1 Ce n'est pas du tout de mon goût.
   (a) *Cela ne m'intéresse pas non plus.*
   (b) *Tu vas prendre ton goûter.*
   (c) *Alors tu y prends beaucoup de plaisir.*

2 Il est enragé de la pêche.
   (a) *Je ne savais pas qu'il s'y intéressait à ce point.*
   (b) *Il se fâche quand il va à la pêche.*
   (c) *Oui, il mange trop de pêches.*

3 Je n'aime pas tellement les jeux de société.
   (a) *Non, je n'aime pas sortir en société.*
   (b) *Ça peut occuper une soirée en famille quand même.*
   (c) *Moi, j'en suis enragé aussi.*

4 Tu aimes la lecture?
   (a) *Oui, c'était bien.*
   (b) *Cela aura lieu dans l'amphithéâtre.*
   (c) *Je lis un roman de temps en temps.*

C Questions orales

1 Comment occupez-vous vos loisirs quand vous êtes à la maison?
2 Qu'est-ce qu'on fait dans un foyer de jeunes?
3 Qu'avez-vous fait samedi dernier?
4 Est-ce que vous aimez la lecture? Qu'est-ce que vous lisez?
5 Est-ce que vous vous intéressez à la musique? Est-ce que vous jouez d'un instrument?

le foyer de jeunes	youth club	la moto	motorbike
le cassettophone	cassette player	aller à la pêche	to go fishing
le groupe pop	pop group	bavarder	to chat
le timbre	stamp	jouer aux cartes	to play cards
le vélo (moteur)	bike (moped)		

6 Cinéma, théâtre, télévision, radio

1 Les séances de **cinéma** commencent **tard** dans la soirée en France.

1 **Cinema** performances start **late** in the evening in France.

2 Au **guichet** on prend des billets pour le parterre ou le balcon.

2 At the **box office** you get tickets for the stalls or the balcony.

3 On offre un pourboire à l'ouvreuse qui vous conduit à votre **place**.

3 A tip is offered to the usherette who shows you to your **seat**.

4 J'adore les **films** d'espionnage, les films d'épouvante et les dessins animés.

4 I love spy **films**, horror films and cartoons.

5 Les westerns font toujours recette, mais ils ne plaisent pas à **tout le monde**.

5 Westerns are always a box-office success but they don't appeal to **everybody**.

6 John Travolta est ma vedette préférée – je **viens de voir** son dernier film.

6 John Travolta is my favourite star – I've **just seen** his latest film.

7 A la télé les meilleures émissions passent très tard à l'écran quand je **dors** devant le téléviseur!

7 On telly the best programmes are on late when I'm **asleep** in front of the set!

8 Les feuilletons policiers m'intriguent surtout quand le complot est compliqué.

8 Police thriller serials fascinate me especially when the plot is complicated.

9 A la radio les **journaux d'informations** et les reportages documentaires m'intéressent surtout.

9 On the radio **news bulletins** and documentary programmes interest me more than anything.

10 Quelquefois des **pièces de théâtre** sont diffusées en direct.

10 Sometimes **plays** are broadcast live.

11 La **musique** d'ambiance diffusée par certains postes ne me plaît pas du tout.

11 I don't enjoy the background **music** put out by some radio stations.

12 Un animateur devrait avoir un certain style et être plein d'esprit.

12 A disc-jockey should have a certain style and be very witty.

détester	to hate	prendre un billet	book a ticket
faire la queue	to queue up	(d'avance)	(in advance)
complet	full up	se terminer	to finish come to an end

A Translate into French

1 He had booked three seats in the balcony.   2 They had to queue up to get the tickets at the box-office.   3 The man decided to offer the usherette a tip.   4 He showed her his ticket and she showed him to his seat.   5 He was sleeping in front of the set when the programme started.   6 The performance ended at midnight.

B Complétez la phrase

1 Le film principal a commencé — dans la soirée, à 9.30.

   (a) *en retard*

   (b) *tôt*

   (c) *tard*

2 Il est allé — pour prendre quatre places.

   (a) *à l'ouvreuse*

   (b) *au parterre*

   (c) *au guichet*

3 Tu vois les gens sortent. La séance vient de —.

   (a) *te voir*

   (b) *commencer*

   (c) *se terminer*

C Qu'est-ce qu'on répondrait?

1 A quelle heure est-ce que le journal passe à l'écran?

   (a) *Après ce reportage.*

   (b) *Cela s'est passé hier.*

   (c) *Je lis le journal à sept heures.*

2 Tu as entendu? C'est complet au parterre.

   (a) *Je vais m'étendre par terre.*

   (b) *Alors la séance est terminée.*

   (c) *Il reste des places au balcon?*

3 Quel complot!

   (a) *Cela manque de réalité, je dois l'avouer.*

   (b) *Mais c'est toujours complet!*

   (c) *C'est moi le complice.*

D Questions orales

1 Préférez-vous le cinéma ou la télé? Pourquoi?

2 Quels genres de films aimez-vous? Pourquoi?

3 Qu'est-ce que vous avez regardé à la télé le weekend?

4 Qu'est-ce que vous aimez écouter à la radio?

5 Racontez le complot d'une pièce que vous avez vue.

7 Les sports

1 J'essaie de me maintenir en forme en faisant du sport.

1 I try to keep fit by doing some sport.

2 Le samedi je joue au hockey pour l'équipe de l'école.

2 On Saturdays I play hockey for the school team.

3 Nous sommes obligés de faire beaucoup d'entraînement pour améliorer notre performance.

3 We have to do a lot of training to improve our performance.

4 Avant tout, c'est l'élément de compétition que je trouve passionnant.

4 Above all, it's the element of competition which I find exciting.

5 Mes parents assistent souvent aux matches pour m'encourager.

5 My parents frequently attend the matches to support me.

6 En été je fais de l'athlétisme et je joue au tennis sur gazon.

6 In summer I do athletics and play lawn tennis.

7 J'aime toutes les activités en plein air – j'aime beaucoup faire de la voile par exemple.

7 I like all out-of-door activities – for instance, I enjoy sailing tremendously.

8 Les sports violents – et quelquefois dangereux – comme la lutte et la boxe ne m'attirent pas du tout.

8 Violent – and sometimes dangerous – sports like wrestling and boxing don't appeal to me at all.

9 Mon frère est supporter de football. Son équipe est en tête de la première division.

9 My brother is a football supporter. His team is at the top of the first division.

10 Mon père aime regarder les courses d'auto à la télé, surtout quand on passe la ligne d'arrivée.

10 My father likes watching the motor racing on telly, especially when they're crossing the finishing line.

11 J'attends avec beaucoup de plaisir la saison des sports d'hiver.

11 I'm looking forward to the winter sports season.

12 J'adore le ski de descente, le ski de fond et le patinage.

12 I adore downhill and cross-country skiing, and skating.

le cyclisme	cycling	la partie	game
le jeu	match	la tenue de sports	sports clothes
le joueur	player	battre	to beat
le matériel	equipment	gagner	to win
le prix	prize	perdre	to lose

A Translate into French

1 He was playing tennis when his parents arrived. **2** The team from Strasbourg beat the team from Metz. **3** They would lose the match but still win a prize. **4** They used to support their daughter at the hockey matches. **5** We're going to watch the match on telly.

B Compréhension

L'homme de la rue des années soixante-dix n'est pas toujours très disposé à participer activement au sport. Il regarde le sport à la télé et même assiste volontiers aux rencontres sportives, mais il aime moins pratiquer le sport et montre peu d'enthousiasme pour l'entraînement qui pourrait développer ses talents. Cela est un peu étonnant étant donné l'amélioration des facilités sportives au cours des dix années qui viennent de s'écouler. La popularité toujours croissant du footing est peut-être un signe plus positif d'un changement d'attitude.

1 (a) Les vieillards ne sont pas disposés à faire du sport dans la rue.
  (b) L'homme de soixante-dix ans a de mauvaises dispositions.
  (c) L'homme moyen s'intéresse souvent à l'aspect passif du sport.
  (d) L'homme moyen s'intéresse à l'aspect positif du sport.

2 (a) On préfère souvent rester spectateur.
  (b) On aime aider les joueurs.
  (c) On a beaucoup de bonne volonté.
  (d) On n'aime pas le sport à la télé.

3 (a) On aime les courses à la montre.
  (b) On montre assez d'enthousiasme pour l'entraînement.
  (c) On développe ses talents.
  (d) Si on s'entraînait, les performances seraient meilleures.

4 (a) L'attitude envers la participation active va changer.
  (b) Il y avait plus de possibilités de faire du sport.
  (c) Les facilités sportives étaient meilleures il y a dix ans.
  (d) Ceux qui font du footing mangent des croissants.

C Questions orales

1 Quelle est la différence entre une balle et un ballon?
2 Quels sports peut-on pratiquer dans les Alpes?
3 Décrivez la tenue de votre équipe de hockey/football.
4 Que savez-vous du Tour de France?
5 Expliquez ce que vous feriez pour organiser une partie de tennis/un match de football.

8 La ville

1 J'habite un quartier résidentiel à dix **kilomètres** du centre de la **ville**.

1 I live in a residential district ten **kilometres** from the centre of the **town**.

2 Ma **sœur** aînée habite un petit **village** de quelques centaines d'habitants.

2 My elder **sister** lives in a **village** with a few hundred inhabitants.

3 Je **préfère** la ville parce qu'on a plus de distractions à sa disposition.

3 I **prefer** the town because there's more entertainment available.

4 Nous disposons, par exemple, d'une **bibliothèque**, d'un **cinéma** et d'un **théâtre**.

4 We have at our disposal, for example, a **library**, a **cinema** and a **theatre**.

5 Le **samedi** la **rue** principale est très affairée à cause des **personnes** qui font leurs **achats**.

5 On **Saturdays** the main **street** is very crowded because of **people** doing their **shopping**.

6 La **place du marché** est entourée de **magasins**.

6 The **market square** is surrounded by big **shops**.

7 Les **bâtiments** les plus anciens, la **mairie**, la cathédrale et le tribunal, datent du seizième siècle.

7 The oldest **buildings**, the **town hall**, cathedral and law courts, date back to the sixteenth century.

8 Pour les touristes il **y a** plusieurs endroits qui sont d'intérêt historique.

8 For tourists there are several places which are of historical interest.

9 J'aimerais **aller** en Angleterre pour **voir** les petites **maisons** aux **toits** de chaume . . .

9 I would like **to go** to England to see the **little** houses with thatched **roofs** . . .

10 et les **châteaux forts** qu'on voit sur les **cartes postales**.

10 and the **castles** which you see on **postcards**.

11 J'ai un cousin qui a trouvé un emploi dans l'usine . . .

11 I have a cousin who's found a job in the factory . . .

12 qu'on vient d'implanter dans la zone industrielle dans la banlieue de la ville.

12 which they've just set up in the industrial estate on the outskirts of the town.

un hôpital	hospital	une église	church
le parc	park	la gare routière	bus station
le trottoir	pavement	beaucoup de monde	lots of people

A Translate into French

1 Our house is situated in a residential district. **2** We live five kilometres from the town centre. **3** Every Saturday several hundred tourists go on a guided tour of the cathedral. **4** There were lots of people on the pavement.

B Compréhension

J'habite un petit village dont la population indigène n'est pas tellement nombreuse, mais qui est envahie par des touristes pendant les weekends. Ils ont la possibilité de faire une visite guidée de l'église le dimanche, par exemple. Mais très peu de distractions restent à la disposition des habitants. Tout franchement j'aimerais voir plus d'animation culturelle et moins de touristes.

1 (a) C'est un village très fréquenté par les touristes.
  (b) La population est nombreuse.
  (c) Il y a une invasion de touristes à tous les moments.
  (d) Le village est moins affairé le weekend.
2 (a) Les habitants sont à la disposition des touristes.
  (b) Le narrateur reste dans le village pour se distraire.
  (c) Il n'y a pas grand'chose à faire pour les résidents.
  (d) Il y a très peu à faire pour les touristes.
3 (a) Le narrateur préférerait un milieu plus stimulant.
  (b) Le narrateur aime les touristes parce qu'ils sont animés.
  (c) Le narrateur voit plus d'animation culturelle.
  (d) Les touristes cherchent un certain niveau de culture.

C Questions orales

1 Où travaillent la plupart des habitants de cette ville/la ville la plus proche?
2 Quelles sont les principales distractions de cette ville?
3 Décrivez le centre de cette ville/la ville la plus proche.
4 Donnez quelques détails de l'histoire de cette ville.
5 A votre avis, quels changements verra-t-on dans la ville d'ici vingt ans?
6 Décrivez un bâtiment intéressant que vous connaissez dans cette ville/dans la région.
7 Q'est-ce que c'est qu'une gare routière?
8 Quels sont les problèmes d'un automobiliste dans une grande ville?

être situé/se trouver to be (located)
faire une visite guidée to go on a guided tour

9 Les magasins (1)

1 Samedi dernier j'ai dû **faire des achats** pour maman en ville.

2 On y **trouve** toutes sortes de **boutiques**, depuis le petit commerçant jusqu'au **centre commercial**.

3 D'abord je suis passé à la **boucherie** pour acheter trois côtelettes de mouton.

4 A côté il y a une **bonne charcuterie** qui se spécialise dans le saucisson sec.

5 Ensuite **je suis allé** à la **pharmacie** avec une ordonnance.

6 A la **crémerie** – du **lait**, un pot de **crème**, un demi-kilo de **beurre** et une douzaine d'**œufs**.

7 A la **librairie-papeterie** j'ai acheté un **livre de poche**.

8 Au magasin de disques j'ai **choisi** le dernier tube de Wings comme **cadeau** pour ma **sœur**.

9 A la **pâtisserie** je me suis payé un baba au rhum.

10 A la **boulangerie** – deux grandes **baguettes**.

11 Pour ma dernière course j'ai acheté un mandat postal et des **timbres** au **bureau de poste**.

12 Après avoir vérifié ma **monnaie, je suis rentré** à la **maison**.

1 Last Saturday I had **to do some shopping** for mum in town.

2 You **find** all sorts of **shops** there, from the corner shop to the **shopping centre**.

3 First of all I called at the **butcher's** to buy three lamb chops.

4 Next door there's a **good delicatessen** which specializes in cooked sausage.

5 Then **I went** to the **chemist's** with a prescription.

6 At the **dairy shop – milk**, a pot of **cream**, half a kilo of **butter** and a dozen **eggs**.

7 At the **bookshop and stationer's** I bought a **paperback**.

8 At the record shop I **chose** Wings' latest hit as a **present** for my **sister**.

9 At the **confectioner's** I treated myself to a rum baba.

10 At the **baker's** – two large **French sticks**.

11 For my last errand I bought a postal order and some **stamps** at the **post office**.

12 After checking my **change** I **went home**.

le chocolat	chocolate	la liste	list
le gâteau	cake	la vitrine	shop window

A Translate into English

Mme Orteil était sur le point de compléter sa liste d'achats – elle avait presque oublié la bouteille d'Ambre Solaire pour le départ en vacances. Après avoir achevé la liste, elle s'est mise en route pour la grand'rue. Le boucher l'a saluée quand elle est entrée dans sa boutique – elle était une cliente habituée:

– Bonjour madame. En quoi puis-je vous servir?
– Un bon morceau de bœuf – à peu près un kilo – mais pas trop gras s'il vous plaît.
– Ça vous va comme ca?
– C'est parfait.
– Et avec ça madame?
– C'est tout merci.
  Puis elle est passée à l'épicerie.
– Je voudrais un demi-kilo de choux de Bruxelles, s'il vous plaît.
– Désolé, madame, je n'ai plus de choux de Bruxelles.
– Alors je prends deux choux-fleurs. Ils sont combien la pièce?
– Deux francs dix, madame.

Puisqu'elle voulait acheter un cadeau de noce pour une amie, elle a pénétré dans un grand magasin. Elle avait vraiment l'embarras du choix. Dans le rayon 'articles de ménage' elle a vu une cafetière électrique – mais avec une étiquette de 160 francs! Elle aurait dû trouver quelque chose de moins cher, mais son amie apprécierait ce joli cadeau. Elle a fait son achat et a expliqué à la vendeuse qu'elle allait l'offrir comme cadeau. La vendeuse a emballé la cafetière dans un papier spécial.

B Questions orales

1 Que faites-vous quand le médecin vous donne une ordonnance?
2 Quels sont les services que vous offre un bureau de poste?
3 Qu'avez vous fait de votre argent de poche la semaine dernière?
4 Dites ce que vous faites quand vous achetez un disque.
5 Quelles difficultés rencontre-t-on quand on veut acheter un cadeau d'anniversaire?

le journal	newspaper	dépenser (sur)	to spend on
le magasin	(large) shop	emballer	to wrap up
le magazine	magazine	garder	to keep
le paquet	parcel, packet	100 grammes de	100 grams of
la glace	ice cream	un litre de	a litre of

10 Les magasins (2)

1 De nos jours la petite **boutique** du coin doit faire concurrence à l'hypermarché.

2 L'hypermarché offre un grand choix de produits et un parking **gratuit**.

3 Des économies de temps et d'**argent** – s'il n'y a pas trop de monde à la **caisse**!

4 **Moi**, je **préfère** le service personnel du petit **marchand derrière** son comptoir.

5 Le **vendeur** ou la **vendeuse** peut vous conseiller, vous bavarder.

6 On livre certains produits à domicile (mais pas le **lait**).

7 Un **marché** a lieu le **jeudi** et le **samedi** dans notre **ville**.

8 Les marchands se tiennent derrière leurs étalages.

9 On peut examiner les produits en vente. Ils sont bien frais!

10 Les ménagères françaises n'aiment pas tellement les produits **en boîte** ou surgelés.

11 Au **supermarché** les prix sont moins élevés – mais c'est moins animé.

12 Si vous préférez la chaleur humaine, passez chez votre commerçant du quartier.

1 Nowadays the corner **shop** has to compete with the hypermarket.

2 The hypermarket offers a wide choice of products and **free** parking.

3 Savings in time and **money** – if there aren't too many people at the **checkout**.

4 **I prefer** the personal service of the small **shopkeeper behind** his counter.

5 The **salesman** or **saleswoman** can give you advice, chat to you.

6 Certain products are delivered to your home (but not **milk**).

7 There is a **market** in our **town** on **Thursdays** and **Saturdays**.

8 The traders stand behind their stalls.

9 You can examine the products on sale. They really are fresh!

10 French housewives are not very keen on **tinned** or frozen products.

11 At the **supermarket** the prices are lower – but it's less lively.

12 If you prefer the human touch, call in at your local shop.

le client	customer (male)
la cliente	customer (female)
le panier	basket
la banane	banana
une orange	orange
les heures d'ouverture	opening hours

la pomme	apple
peser	to weigh
servir	to serve
fermé	closed
ouvert	open

A Translate into French

1 The saleswoman was standing behind the counter. 2 The lady customer entered the shop. 3 There were lots of people at the checkout. 4 The market used to be held on Mondays and Fridays. 5 She examined the apples and decided to buy a kilo of them. 6 She put the two kilos of oranges and the kilo of bananas in her shopping bag. 7 She said goodbye to the shopkeeper and left the shop. 8 The tradesman served the customer.

B De quoi est-ce qu'on parle?

1 Surface de vente en plein air où les produits sont exposés sur des étalages.
2 La personne qui vend les produits dans un magasin.
3 La personne qui achète les produits dans un magasin.
4 Une sorte de table derrière laquelle se tient le commerçant dans un magasin.
5 L'endroit où on paie ses achats dans un hypermarché ou un supermarché.

C Qu'est-ce qu'on répondrait?

1 Est-ce que vous livrez à domicile?
   (a) *Oui, j'ai des livres chez moi.*
   (b) *Oui, samedi j'ai fait la livraison chez vous.*
   (c) *Oui, le mardi et le vendredi.*
2 Tu vois tous ces fruits exposés sur l'étalage?
   (a) *Oui, c'est dommage.*
   (b) *Oui, je suis allé à l'exposition.*
   (c) *Quel embarras du choix! Je vais demander un conseil au marchand.*
3 Il y a beaucoup de monde. On devra attendre longtemps.
   (a) *Oui, je repasserai plus tard.*
   (b) *Oui, on peut faire des économies de temps.*
   (c) *Oui, il fallait faire la queue.*

D Questions orales

1 Est-ce qu'on livre le lait à domicile en France?
2 Que fait une vendeuse?
3 Quels sont les avantages du supermarché pour les ménagères?
4 Vous faites les magasins avec cinquante livres en poche. Imaginez votre après-midi.
5 Faites la description d'un grand magasin que vous connaissez.

11 L'école

1 Je suis **élève** depuis cinq ans d'un CES de 2000 étudiants.

1 I've been a **pupil** in a comprehensive of 2000 students for five years.

2 C'est une **école** mixte dont la plupart des élèves sont sérieux.

2 It's a mixed **school**, whose pupils are mainly responsible.

3 Il y en a quand même qui font des bêtises de temps en temps.

3 All the same there are some who act the fool from time to time.

4 Je suis en seconde et j'étudie plusieurs matières : français, maths, anglais, histoire, géographie.

4 I'm in the fifth year and study several subjects: French, maths, English, history, geography.

5 A la fin de l'**année** je passe mon BES.

5 At the end of the **year** I'm taking CSE/O level exams.

6 La journée commence à 8h.30 et chaque **cours dure** une **heure** normalement.

6 The day begins at 8.30 and each **lesson lasts** an **hour** normally.

7 A dix heures il y a une petite pause et puis cela reprend à dix heures dix.

7 At ten there's a short break, then we resume at ten-past ten.

8 Entre **midi** et deux heures on peut **déjeuner** dans la cantine.

8 Between **twelve** and two o'clock you can **have lunch** in the canteen.

9 La nourriture n'est pas tellement bonne; ceux qui n'habitent pas loin rentrent **chez eux**.

9 The food isn't particularly good; those who don't live far away go **home**.

10 Les cours recommencent à deux heures et se terminent vers cinq heures avec une seule récréation.

10 Lessons start again at two o'clock and finish around five with a single break.

11 En France nous ne sommes pas obligés de porter l'uniforme scolaire.

11 We don't have to wear school uniform in France.

12 En général le règlement est moins strict et l'atmosphère moins compassée depuis 1968.

12 In general the rules have been less strict and the atmosphere less formal since 1968.

le bic	biro
le feutre	felt tip pen
le lycée	grammar school
le professeur	teacher

la cour	school yard
l'éducation physique	PE
les sciences	science

A Compréhension

En principe je suis un élève sage qui prends mes études au sérieux (je dois passer mon BES en fin de l'année scolaire) bien que je me conduise mal par moments. C'est l'anglais qui est ma matière préférée. Notre prof d'anglais est assez sévère mais pas trop compassé, de sorte que personne ne fasse de bêtises en classe et le groupe travaille bien. La journée scolaire est longue et j'apprécie les petites pauses qui nous permettent de nous décontracter après des séances rigoureuses de travail.

1 (a) L'élève fait des bêtises de temps en temps.
  (b) L'élève se conduit mal à tous moments.
  (c) L'élève se conduit bien de temps en temps.
  (d) L'élève se conduit bien tout le temps.

2 (a) L'élève sait qu'il doit se présenter à un examen.
  (b) L'élève sait qu'il va réussir à un examen.
  (c) L'élève a passé son examen en fin d'année.
  (d) L'élève a réussi à son examen de fin d'année scolaire.

3 (a) Le prof d'anglais est trop compassé.
  (b) Le prof d'anglais n'est pas tellement compassé.
  (c) Le prof d'anglais est trop sévère.
  (d) Le prof d'anglais n'est pas assez compassé.

4 (a) L'élève aime se décontracter pendant les cours rigoureux.
  (b) L'élève est fatigué après son long voyage à l'école.
  (c) L'élève aime les récréations.
  (d) L'élève déteste les séances rigoureuses de travail.

B Questions orales

1 Combien d'élèves y a-t-il dans votre classe et dans l'école?
2 Prenez-vous votre repas de midi à l'école? Pourquoi/pas?
3 Quel jour de la semaine préférez-vous? Pourquoi?
4 Est-ce que vous êtes obligé de porter l'uniforme scolaire?
5 Est-ce que votre uniforme scolaire vous plaît? Pourquoi/pas?
6 Aimeriez-vous être professeur? Pourquoi/pas?
7 Décrivez une journée typique à l'école.
8 Que voudriez-vous changer dans votre vie scolaire? Pourquoi?
9 En quoi la vie scolaire en France est-elle différente de la nôtre?

se conduire	to behave	réussir à un examen	to pass an exam
bien/mal	well/badly		
punir	to punish	sage	well behaved
préféré	favourite	sévère	strict

12 Au-delà de l'école

1 A la fin de l'année scolaire je voudrais **entrer en** première pour préparer des examens au niveau avancé.

1 At the end of the school year I would like to **go into** the sixth form to prepare exams at advanced level.

2 Quant à la faculté, je ne sais pas qu'en penser moi-même.

2 As far as university is concerned, I'm not clear in my mind about it.

3 Beaucoup de mes **amis** vont **quitter** l'école en **juillet** pour trouver un **emploi**.

3 Lots of my **friends** are going **to leave** school in **July** to find a **job**.

4 Malheureusement le chômage est très répandu dans cette région.

4 Unfortunately unemployment is widespread in this region.

5 En même temps il y a un manque de main-d'œuvre qualifiée.

5 At the same time there's a shortage of skilled labour.

6 Peu de **jeunes gens** semblent s'intéresser à **devenir** ingénieur, par exemple.

6 **Few youngsters** seem to be interested in **becoming** engineers, for example.

7 On est attiré plutôt vers les secteurs non-productifs.

7 People are attracted rather towards the non-productive sectors.

8 Est-ce que c'est à cause des heures, des conditions de travail ou du salaire?

8 Is it because of the hours, working conditions or wages?

9 Si vous voulez exercer une profession – **médecin**, avocat ou **professeur**, par exemple . . .

9 If you want to practise a career – **doctor**, barrister or **teacher**, for example . . .

10 on exige un niveau très élevé de qualifications et de formation.

10 a high level of qualifications and training is demanded.

11 Ceux qui ont l'occasion de poursuivre une carrière qui leur plaît . . .

11 Those who have the opportunity to follow a career which they enjoy . . .

12 mises à part les considérations financières, ont vraiment de la chance.

12 putting aside financial considerations, are really lucky.

le bureau   office

le conducteur   driver

A Translate into French

1 He became a doctor. **2** He will find a job in a factory. **3** She was interested in becoming a primary school teacher. **4** My mother is an office worker. **5** When I leave school I want to be an engineer.

B Qu'est-qu'on répondrait?

1 Peu de gens semblent s'intéresser au travail d'usine.
  (a) *C'est pour cela qu'il y a tant de chômage.*
  (b) *Oui, le travail d'usine est intéressant.*
  (c) *Oui, cela ne les attire pas.*

2 Mon père est instituteur.
  (a) *Je n'aimerais pas m'occuper toujours de jeunes enfants.*
  (b) *Je n'aime pas les institutions.*
  (c) *Je n'aimerais pas la vie de bureau.*

3 Mon frère travaille à la chaîne.
  (a) *J'aimerais travailler en plein air aussi.*
  (b) *Le travail d'usine peut être monotone.*
  (c) *Depuis quand est-il en prison?*

4 Mon emploi me plaît beaucoup sauf la paie.
  (a) *Tu as de la chance; tu es bien payé et content de ton emploi.*
  (b) *Je n'aime pas mon emploi non plus.*
  (c) *Il y a d'autres considérations que le salaire.*

C Questions orales

1 Qu'avez-vous l'intention de faire quand vous quitterez l'école?
2 Quels sont les avantages et les inconvénients des études de première?
3 Aimeriez-vous aller à la faculté? Pourquoi/pas?
4 Quels sont les avantages et les inconvénients d'exercer une profession?
5 Qu'est-ce qui influence votre choix de carrière – uniquement le niveau du salaire?

le caissier la caissière	cashier	un(e) employé(e) de magasin	shop worker
le gérant	manager	le soldat	soldier

un(e) instituteur
  (-trice)
	primary school
	  teacher
		une usine	factory

le mécanicien	mechanic	travailler à la
		  chaîne
			to work on the
			  production line

un ouvrier	workman	habile	skilful

13 Les transports

1 En **avion** la durée du vol est souvent brève grâce à la vitesse élevée . . .

1 In a **plane** the length of the flight is often short thanks to the high speed . . .

2 mais il faut faire la queue pour passer la douane.

2 but you have to queue up to go through customs.

3 A un **aéroport** comme Charles de Gaulle, des centaines d'avions atterrissent ou décollent par jour aux périodes d'affluence.

3 At an **airport** like Charles de Gaulle, hundreds of planes land or take off every day at busy periods.

4 Aux **heures de pointe** la circulation urbaine est dense et souvent perturbée.

4 In the **rush hour** city traffic is heavy and often held up.

5 Les **autobus** et les rames de métro sont bondés de **voyageurs**.

5 **Buses** and tube trains are packed with **passengers**.

6 A Paris un réseau urbain modernisé dessert le centre et la proche banlieue.

6 In Paris a modernized urban tube network serves the centre and immediate suburbs.

7 C'est un système à tarif unique très pratique pour les banlieusards.

7 It's a flat rate fare system, very handy for commuters.

8 En **autobus** le **prix du billet** varie selon la distance parcourue.

8 By **bus** the **fare** varies according to the distance travelled.

9 Les transports en commun peuvent offrir des économies d'**argent** et d'énergie.

9 Public transport can offer savings in **money** and energy.

10 Le **vélo** est un moyen de transport peu coûteux qui vous fait du bien par-dessus le marché.

10 The **bike** is an inexpensive means of transport which does you good into the bargain.

11 A l'avenir les trajets urbains se feront en **voiture** électrique ou par monorail peut-être.

11 In the future trips within towns will be made in electric **cars** or by monorail perhaps.

12 Des hélicoptères feront la navette entre le centre-ville et l'aéroport.

12 Helicopters will run a shuttle service between the town centre and the airport.

un arrêt	stop	le car	coach
le canot	small boat	le conducteur	driver

A Translate into French
1 They queued up to go through customs. 2 He bought a ticket from the driver. 3 He took a bus from the airport to the town centre.
4 I made the journey by coach. 5 She got on the bus. 6 Mr and Mrs Delage had to get off the train immediately.

B Compréhension
Les banlieusards doivent faire face à de multiples inconvénients au cours de leur trajet domicile-emploi. Il faut faire la queue à l'arrêt avant de monter dans un autobus souvent bondé, dont l'horaire est souvent perturbé selon la densité de la circulation. Si vous habitez une grande agglomération desservie par un chemin de fer souterrain, cela peut vous offrir une économie de temps aux heures d'affluence. Pour l'avenir on pense aux voyages par monorail plutôt qu'en autobus ou métro.

1 (a) Les banlieusards trouvent difficile de suivre un cours.
  (b) Les banlieusards doivent surmonter certaines difficultés deux fois par jour.
  (c) Le nombre de banlieusards se multiplie.
  (d) Les banlieusards sont employés à domicile.
2 (a) La durée du trajet en autobus dépend de la circulation.
  (b) Les voyageurs doivent bondir pour être à l'heure.
  (c) Les autobus ne sont jamais à l'heure.
  (d) Les autobus sont à l'heure surtout aux moments d'affluence.
3 (a) Les voyages ont été faits par monorail.
  (b) Les habitants des grands centres de population sont mieux desservis dans un certain sens.
  (c) Les gens riches peuvent prendre le métro.
  (d) On prend le monorail plutôt que l'autobus ou le train.

C Questions orales
1 Que se passe-t-il quand on débarque dans un pays étranger?
2 Décrivez brièvement un voyage que vous avez fait.
3 Quels sont les avantages des excursions à vélo?
4 Comment envisagez-vous les moyens de transport en l'an 2000?
5 Quelles sont les grandes différences entre les chemins de fer souterrains métropolitains à Londres et à Paris?
6 Quel moyen de transport préférez-vous et pourquoi?

le navire	ship	faire un voyage	to go on a journey
le passeport	passport	monter dans	to get on
le vélomoteur	moped	prendre un	to buy a
descendre de	to get off (bus, train)	billet à . . .	ticket from . . .

14 Les chemins de fer

1 Les **voyages** en chemin de fer sont en principe **rapides** et **confortables**.

1 **Journeys** by rail are in theory **quick** and **comfortable**.

2 On prend son **billet** au guichet – première ou deuxième classe, aller simple ou aller et retour.

2 You buy your **ticket** at the ticket office – first or second class, single or return.

3 Il n'y a plus de contrôleurs à l'**entrée** du **quai**; vous compostez vous-même votre **billet**, en vous servant d'une machine prévue à cet effet.

3 There are no more ticket inspectors at the **platform entrance**; you cancel your own **ticket** in a machine designed for this purpose.

4 Les **voitures** les plus récentes ont des portières qui s'ouvrent et se ferment automatiquement.

4 The latest **carriages** have doors which open and close automatically.

5 Si vous voyagez la **nuit**, vous pouvez réserver une couchette.

5 If you're travelling by **night**, you can reserve a couchette berth.

6 Vous avez **faim** ou **soif**? Passez au **buffet** ou à la voiture-restaurant.

6 **Hungry** or **thirsty**? Go along to the **buffet** or restaurant car.

7 Les **gares** offrent plusieurs facilités aux **voyageurs** – services de consigne ou de change.

7 **Stations** offer several amenities to **travellers** – left-luggage and money changing services.

8 Au **bureau de renseignements** on se renseigne sur l'horaire des trains.

8 At the **information office** you find out about train times.

9 Si vos **bagages** sont **lourds**, cherchez un chariot ou même un **porteur**.

9 If your **luggage** is **heavy**, look for a trolley or even a **porter**.

10 On peut louer des voitures sans chauffeur dans certaines **gares** principales.

10 Self-drive cars can be hired at certain main **stations**.

11 Les ferry-boats et les aéroglisseurs de la SNCF font la navette entre Douvres et Calais.

11 French Railways ferries and hovercrafts ply between Dover and Calais.

12 Le tunnel projeté réduira de plusieurs **heures** le parcours Londres–Paris.

12 The planned tunnel will cut the London–Paris journey by several **hours**.

A Translate into French

1 The man bought a second-class return for Lyon at the ticket office.
2 The train departed from the station on time. 3 I don't like travelling at night. 4 Because he was thirsty he went along to the buffet car.
5 The passenger enquired about the train times. 6 He had hired a car. 7 The two girls got into the carriage. 8 The three boys got off the train at Calais. 9 The train arrived late. 10 The porter was carrying two suitcases.

B Qu'est-ce qu'on répondrait?

1 Le train est sur le point de partir.
   (a) *Attention aux barrières!*
   (b) *Attention au quai!*
   (c) *Attention aux portières!*
2 Vous préférez voyager la nuit?
   (a) *J'ai voyagé cette nuit.*
   (b) *Je prendrai une couchette.*
   (c) *Je trouve qu'il y a moins de monde.*
3 Tu sais quand partira le train?
   (a) *Oui, je me suis renseigné sur l'horaire.*
   (b) *Oui, il est parti à deux heures.*
   (c) *Oui, j'irai au bureau de renseignements.*
4 Nous avons dû rater le train – il est déjà deux heures passées.
   (a) *Mais il ne part qu'à deux heures vingt-cinq.*
   (b) *Oui, nous allons passer à la gare.*
   (c) *Oui, les trains sont dépassés maintenant.*
5 La durée du voyage sera réduite de trois heures.
   (a) *Alors il durera trois heures de plus.*
   (b) *Alors sept heures au lieu de dix.*
   (c) *Alors trois heures plutôt que quatre heures.*

C Questions orales

1 Quels sont les avantages des voyages en chemin de fer?
2 Quels préparatifs feriez-vous si vous deviez faire un voyage en chemin de fer?
3 Décrivez un voyage que vous avez fait en train.
4 Qu'est-ce que c'est qu'un bureau de consigne dans une gare?
5 Quels seraient les avantages d'un tunnel sous la Manche?

le compartiment	compartment	la voie	track
le départ	departure	rater	to miss
une arrivée	arrival		

15 La voiture (1)

1 **Avant de** faire un **voyage** en France en **voiture** il y a plusieurs préparatifs à faire.

1 **Before** going on a **car journey** to France there are several preparations to be made.

2 Il faut **penser à** l'entretien, les niveaux d'**huile**, **d'eau** et **d'essence** par exemple.

2 You have **to think of** maintenance, the levels of **oil**, **water** and **petrol** for instance.

3 Vérifiez la pression des **pneus**, y compris le pneu de rechange.

3 Check the **tyre** pressures, including the spare.

4 Consultez le Code de la Route, surtout en ce qui concerne les règles de priorité.

4 Refer to the Highway Code, especially as far as the rules of priority are concerned.

5 N'oubliez pas d'essuyer le pare-brise et les glaces, et de nettoyer les phares et les feux extérieurs.

5 Don't forget to wipe the windscreen and windows, and to clean the headlamps and outside lights.

6 Ne surchargez pas le **coffre**: cela peut avoir un effet sur la tenue de route et les **freins**.

6 Don't overload the **boot**: it can affect the road holding and the **brakes**.

7 Il est obligatoire de porter la ceinture de sécurité pour tous les **voyages**.

7 Wearing seat belts is compulsory for all **journeys**.

8 Ne restez pas trop longtemps au volant; il est très **dangereux** de **conduire** quand on est **fatigué**.

8 Don't stay at the wheel too long; it's very **dangerous** to **drive** when you're **tired**.

9 **Faites le plein** avant de prendre l'autoroute – les pannes sèches sont coûteuses.

9 **Fill your tank** before going on the motorway – running out of petrol is expensive.

10 **Écoutez** les informations routières afin d'éviter des embouteillages ou des perturbations.

10 **Listen** to the traffic news in order to avoid traffic jams or hold-ups.

11 En cas de panne, il vaut mieux **téléphoner** au touring-secours.

11 In case of breakdown, it's better to **ring** for the breakdown service of a motoring organization.

12 S'il s'agit d'une crevaison, remplacez le pneu crevé vous-même.

12 If a puncture is involved, change the punctured tyre yourself.

A Translate into French

1 He always checked the tyres, the oil, water and petrol. 2 They pulled up at a service station. 3 I like to travel on main roads. 4 The taxi driver opened the boot. 5 They parked the car in a car park. 6 She drove for two hours, then got out of the car. 7 The motorist got into his car. 8 He bought twenty litres of 4 star.

B Qu'est-ce qu'on répondrait?

1 Vous allez tomber en panne, monsieur, avec un coffre surchargé comme cela.

   (a) *Oui, je suis tombé en panne.*

   (b) *Mais je suis surchargé de travail.*

   (c) *J'ai une famille nombreuse et une petite voiture.*

2 Faites le plein, s'il vous plaît, et vérifiez les pneus.

   (a) *Oui, monsieur, du super?*

   (b) *Oui, monsieur, le coffre est plein.*

   (c) *Oui, monsieur, il y en a quatre.*

3 Je voudrais le service 'Touring Secours' s'il vous plaît.

   (a) *D'accord, monsieur, au secours!*

   (b) *Qu'est-ce que vous faites comme tour, monsieur?*

   (c) *C'est une panne sèche, moteur, crevaison?*

4 Tu as écouté les informations routières, papa?

   (a) *Je ne m'entends pas avec les routiers.*

   (b) *Oui, les routiers ne sont pas bien informés.*

   (c) *Oui, il y a un embouteillage sur la RN 7, mais ce n'est pas grave.*

5 J'insiste que tu ne restes plus au volant.

   (a) *Je n'ai pas dormi plus de deux minutes au volant.*

   (b) *Tu as raison; je conduis depuis plusieurs heures maintenant.*

   (c) *J'aimerais voler encore quelques moments.*

C Questions orales

1 Que veut dire 'faire le plein' dans une station de service?
2 Quels sont les problèmes d'un automobiliste dans une grande ville?
3 Quels préparatifs feriez-vous si vous deviez faire un voyage en auto?
4 Décrivez un voyage que vous avez fait en voiture.
5 Comment est-ce qu'on peut éviter des embouteillages?

le chauffeur de taxi	taxi driver	arrêter la voiture	to stop the car
le mécanicien	mechanic	descendre de ⎱ la voiture	to get out of/in
le moteur	engine	monter dans ⎰	
l'ordinaire/le super	2/4 star petrol		the car
le parking	car park	garer	to park
la route nationale	main ('A') road	rouler	to travel, go
s'arrêter	to stop, pull up	tomber en panne	to break down

16 La voiture (2)

1 On demande aux **visiteurs en voiture** de rouler **avec prudence**.

1 **Visiting motorists** are asked to drive **carefully**.

2 Si vous faites des bêtises – brûler un feu rouge, ne pas s'arrêter aux passages cloutés . . .

2 If you behave stupidly – going through red lights, not stopping at pedestrian crossings . . .

3 ne vous étonnez pas si vous attrapez une amende.

3 don't be surprised if you get fined.

4 Il vous faut certains documents – le permis de conduire et la feuille d'assurances par exemple.

4 You need certain documents – driving licence and insurance papers, for example.

5 En cas d'accident vous êtes obligé de prévenir **la police**.

5 In the case of accident you are obliged to inform the **police**.

6 S'il y a des blessés, **téléphonez** d'urgence à la police-secours.

6 If people are injured, **telephone** as a matter of urgency the rescue services.

7 Une ambulance devrait **arriver** sur les lieux dans un très bref délai.

7 An ambulance should **arrive** on the scene in a short space of time.

8 Les ambulanciers transporteront les blessés à **l'hôpital** le plus proche.

8 The ambulance men will take the injured to the nearest **hospital**.

9 Les sapeurs-pompiers font partie aussi du service de secours.

9 The fire brigade are also part of the rescue services.

10 Les **enfants** s'égarent très facilement dans une **ville** étrange.

10 **Children** easily get lost in a strange **town**.

11 Adressez-vous au commissariat pour donner un signalement détaillé de votre **enfant**.

11 Report to the police station to give a detailed description of your **child**.

12 Ne vous affolez pas ! **La police** ira à la recherche de l'enfant et vous pourrez bientôt continuer votre **voyage**.

12 Don't panic! **The police** will look for the child and you will soon be able to continue your **journey**.

| le camion | lorry | le fossé | ditch |
| le conducteur | driver | le virage | bend |

A Translate into French
The lorry went through the red light and collided with a large black car. Fortunately nobody was seriously injured and the car driver managed to phone the police. A police car soon arrived and the police-man asked the drivers to show their licences. The driver of the lorry had to go with the policeman to the nearest police station. Later he was fined.

B Writing exercise
Using the vocabulary and phrases you have learned, write the following two essays.

1 Your father's car breaks down in the middle of the night quite a way from a garage. Describe exactly how you coped with the situation.
2 You are involved in a car accident in France. There are some minor injuries. Describe how the accident happened, what you did to get help and what happened when help arrived.

C Complétez la phrase
1 Munis d'un signalement de l'enfant égaré, les agents sont allés —.
    (a) à la gare
    (b) faire des recherches
    (c) à sa recherche
2 La voiture du jeune homme est rentrée dans un arbre. Il aurait dû rouler —.
    (a) plus prudemment
    (b) trop vite
    (c) à 130 kilomètres à l'heure

D Questions orales
1 Votre voiture entre en collision avec un camion. Personne n'est gravement blessé. Qu'est-ce que vous feriez?
2 Vous étiez en vacances en France quand votre petit frère s'est égaré. Qu'est-ce que votre père a fait?
3 Vous voyez un accident grave, où il y a des blessés. Qu'est-ce que vous feriez?

la vitesse	speed	rouler à 100	to do
déraper	to skid	kilomètres	100 k.p.h.
faire venir	to send for	à l'heure	
montrer	to show	gravement	seriously
rentrer dans	to run into,	blessé	injured
	collide with	lentement	slowly

17 Les fêtes

1 Le **premier janvier** on **fête** le nouvel an en faisant des résolutions.

2 Le premier **avril** est le **jour** des poissons d'avril.

3 On a deux jours de **congé** à Pâques.

4 La **fête de Pentecôte** a lieu sept **semaines** plus tard.

5 On danse dans les rues le quatorze juillet – la fête nationale en France.

6 Les grandes vacances scolaires sont **longues**. C'est génial!

7 Le quinze **septembre** est le moment de la **rentrée** scolaire.

8 Mon **anniversaire** est le dix **octobre** – **mardi** prochain.

9 On a huit jours de congé pour les vacances de mi-trimestre.

10 Je m'amuse bien pendant la quinzaine de **Noël**.

11 Les **cadeaux**, les sapins et les chants de Noël me plaisent énormément.

12 Dans la plupart des écoles françaises on a congé le **mercredi après-midi**, mais on travaille le **samedi matin**.

1 On **January 1st** we **celebrate** the New Year by making resolutions.

2 **April** 1st is April Fools' **Day**.

3 People have two days **holiday** at Easter

4 The **Whit holiday** takes place seven **weeks** later.

5 People dance in the street on July 14th – the national holiday in France.

6 The summer holidays are **long**. It's fantastic!

7 **September** 15th is the time for **going back** to school.

8 My **birthday** is the 10th **October** – next **Tuesday**.

9 We have a week's holiday for half-term.

10 I really enjoy the **Christmas** fortnight.

11 I enjoy immensely **presents**, Christmas trees and carols.

12 In the majority of French schools pupils are free on **Wednesday afternoons** but work on **Saturday mornings**.

un agenda	diary	Bonne Année	Happy New Year
le calendrier	calendar	jeudi dernier	last Thursday
le lendemain	the next day	dimanche prochain	next Sunday
la veille	the previous day		
commencer	to begin	le jeudi	on Thursdays
consulter	to consult, refer to	février mars	February March
durer	to last	mai	May
se terminer	to come to an end	juin août	June August
hier	yesterday	novembre	November
demain	tomorrow	décembre	December
Joyeux Noël	Merry Christmas		

A Translate into French

1 He used to have Monday mornings off and work Saturday afternoons. 2 They left the next day. 3 I don't work on Sundays. 4 They decided to celebrate her birthday. 5 The Christmas holidays last a fortnight. 6 The summer holidays had started the previous day. 7 He arrived last Thursday. 8 My holidays will finish on the 31st August. 9 'Merry Christmas!' said Paul. 10 'Happy New Year!' he replied. 11 He consulted his diary. 12 They were consulting the calendar when she arrived.

B Qu'est ce qu'on répondrait?

1 Les grandes vacances sont sur le point de se terminer.
   (a) *C'est génial!*
   (b) *Il nous reste encore quelques jours de congé.*
   (c) *Oui, ils viennent de se terminer.*

2 Tu travailles le samedi?
   (a) *Oui, j'ai travaillé samedi.*
   (b) *Non, je travaille mercredi.*
   (c) *Normalement, mais j'ai congé samedi prochain.*

3 Son anniversaire était samedi dernier.
   (a) *On aurait dû lui offrir un cadeau.*
   (b) *On devait lui envoyer une carte.*
   (c) *On lui offrira un cadeau avant son anniversaire.*

4 Je suis arrivé le 23 et elle était déjà partie le 22.
   (a) *Alors son départ était le lendemain.*
   (b) *Alors son départ était hier.*
   (c) *Alors son départ était la veille.*

5 Ça tombe bien – on aura une quinzaine à Noël.
   (a) *Deux semaines de repos!*
   (b) *Quinze cadeaux de Noël!*
   (c) *Oui, Noël aura quinze ans.*

D Questions orales

1 Comment passez-vous le jour de Noël?
2 Qu'est-ce que vous faites normalement pour fêter votre anniversaire?
3 Combien de jours y a-t-il au mois de février?
4 Quelle est la durée des différentes vacances dans cette école?
5 A quel moment de l'année est-ce que vous aimez prendre vos vacances et pourquoi?

18 Les vacances

1 Les **voyages** à forfait offrent la possibilité de **prix** intéressants aux estivants.

1 Package **holidays** offer holiday makers the possibility of attractive **prices**.

2 Tout est **compris** dans le tarif: voyage, **logement** et assurances.

2 Everything is **included** in the price: travelling, **accommodation** and insurance.

3 En **plein été** les **routes** qui mènent à la **côte** sont très encombrées.

3 In **midsummer** the **roads** leading to the **coast** are very congested.

4 **A cause des** flots de **voitures** il y a toujours des perturbations qui sont pénibles pour les **automobilistes**.

4 **Because of** the streams of **cars** there are always hold-ups which are frustrating for **motorists**.

5 Quand on fait du **camping** on est obligé d'**apporter** tout le nécessaire . . .

5 When you go **camping** you have to **take all** the gear with you . . .

6 une **tente**, des duvets, des **lits** de camp, un réchaud à gaz et la batterie de cuisine.

6 a **tent**, sleeping bags, camp **beds**, a gas burner and kitchen utensils.

7 Les **vacances** au camping ne sont pas luxueuses.

7 **Holidays** on a campsite aren't luxurious.

8 C'est **moins cher** qu'à l'**hôtel** quand même.

8 It's **less expensive** than in a **hotel**, all the same.

9 Ce qui est un peu embêtant, c'est qu'il faut **dresser** la tente en **fin** de journée.

9 What is a little bit annoying is that you have to **pitch** the tent at the **end** of the day.

10 Grâce à l'émancipation des **femmes** . . .

10 Thanks to **women's** liberation . . .

11 ce n'est plus toujours la **mère** de famille qui s'occupe de la **cuisine**.

11 it's no longer always the **mother** of the household who looks after the **cooking**.

12 La **pension** complète dans un hôtel de luxe peut **coûter** un argent fou.

12 Full **board** in a luxury hotel can **cost** the earth.

une agence de voyages	travel agency	la région	region
		la semaine	week
une auberge de jeunesse	youth hostel	faire un échange	to do an exchange
		faire un séjour	to go on a trip

A Translate into French

1 They decided to go on a trip to France. 2 We're going to spend three weeks in the mountains. 3 I did an exchange with a French girl. 4 I spent two enjoyable weeks at a youth hostel. 5 She went into a travel agent's. 6 It was an interesting region.

B Compréhension

En plein été on voit des flots de voitures sur le réseau routier de la France. C'est le moment des grandes vacances pour un grand nombre de familles françaises. Malheureusement leurs départs ne s'étendent que sur deux mois de l'année, à la différence des Anglais dont les vacances s'étalent normalement sur une période de plusieurs mois. Ces habitudes bien françaises provoquent d'énormes problèmes dans le domaine des transports. On n'a qu'à étudier le bilan des accidents pour se rendre compte qu'on conduit négligemment après avoir perdu du temps pris dans un embouteillage. Il est sans doute très difficile de passer toute la journée dans une voiture surchargée de matériel de camping sans devenir impatient.

1 (a) En été on fait le plein.
  (b) En été on trouve un grand nombre de véhicules en circulation.
  (c) En été on ne trouve que des routiers en vacances.
  (d) En été on trouve beaucoup de flots.
2 (a) Beaucoup de Français partent en vacances simultanément.
  (b) Les estivants anglais prennent plusieurs vacances.
  (c) Beaucoup de Français passent leurs vacances d'été en Angleterre.
  (d) Les Anglais sont moins habitués que les Français.
3 (a) Les automobilistes sont chargés de payer un argent fou.
  (b) On prend son temps dans un embouteillage.
  (c) On s'impatiente pendant tous les voyages.
  (d) Il est difficile de garder son calme enfermé longtemps en voiture.

C Questions orales

1 Qu'avez-vous fait pendant les grandes vacances d'été?
2 Où allez-vous passer vos vacances cet été?
3 Où aimeriez-vous passer vos vacances? Pourquoi?
4 Pourquoi beaucoup de gens aiment-ils passer leurs vacances à l'étranger?
5 Quels sont les avantages et les inconvénients des vacances au camping?

passer	to spend (of time)	à l'étranger	abroad
agréable	enjoyable	à la montagne	in the mountains

19 Au bord de la mer

1 Si nous **gagnions** aux pronostics de football, nous aimerions faire une croisière aux Indes.

1 If we **won** the pools, we'd like to go on a cruise to the Indies.

2 En réalité nous devons nous contenter de nos quinze jours **au bord de la mer.**

2 In reality we have to content ourselves with our fortnight **at the seaside.**

3 Nous avons **trouvé** un **beau** coin sur la côte normande.

3 We've **found** a **nice** spot on the Normandy coast.

4 **Mon petit frère** apporte toujours sa canne à pêche.

4 **My little brother** always takes his fishing rod.

5 Il passe toute la matinée sur la jetée à faire de la pêche. Il n'attrape **jamais rien**!

5 He spends all morning fishing on the pier. He **never** catches **anything**!

6 Je **préfère** m'allonger sur la **plage** pour **prendre un bain de soleil.**

6 I **prefer** to stretch out on the **beach** to **sunbathe.**

7 C'est un véritable plaisir de regarder passer les jeunes filles bronzées, à la taille svelte.

7 It's a real treat watching the sunburnt, slim-waisted girls go by.

8 Dans le Midi il y a des plages où les **maillots de bain** ne sont plus de rigueur.

8 In the South of France there are beaches where **swimming costumes** are no longer compulsory.

9 J'aime mieux **me baigner** dans une **piscine.** C'est plus pratique si on veut faire des plongeons.

9 I prefer **swimming** in a **swimming pool.** It's handier if you want to dive.

10 Sur la **plage** on peut pratiquer toute une série de **jeux,** si cela vous tente.

10 On the **beach** you can play a whole series of **games,** if that appeals to you.

11 Les **petits** peuvent faire des **châteaux de sable** ou ramasser des galets ou des coquillages.

11 The **kiddies** can make **sandcastles** or collect pebbles or shells.

12 Pour ceux qui **aiment** faire du canotage, on peut **louer** des pédalos.

12 For those who **like** boating, pedal-boats can be **hired.**

A Translate into French

1 We will spend a fortnight on the south coast of England. 2 They had spent the afternoon fishing. 3 I never used to catch anything. 4 I've just been sunbathing on the beach. 5 She was putting on her swimming costume when it began to rain. 6 They bought an ice cream from the ice-cream seller. 7 The man shouted for help. He was drowning. 8 He couldn't swim. 9 They managed to rescue him. 10 I was getting bored. 11 We enjoyed ourselves during the fortnight at the seaside.

B Qu'est ce qu'on répondrait?

1 Tu as ramassé des galets?
   (a) *Oui, je les trouverai sur la plage.*
   (b) *Oui, près de la jetée.*
   (c) *Oui, tu les a jetés.*

2 Écoute – il y a quelqu'un qui crie au secours!
   (a) *Il se noie.*
   (b) *Il s'est noyé.*
   (c) *Il se noyait.*

3 Est-ce qu'on a pu le sauver?
   (a) *Oui, on lui a lancé une bouée de sauvetage et on a réussi à le sortir de l'eau.*
   (b) *Oui, il s'est sauvé.*
   (c) *Oui, on pourra le sauver si on trouve une bouée de sauvetage.*

C Questions orales

1 Est-ce que vous avez passé des vacances au bord de la mer? Quand et où?

2 Est-ce que vous aimez passer des vacances au bord de la mer? Pourquoi/pas?

3 Est-ce que vous préférez des baignades de mer ou de piscine? Pourquoi?

le marchand de glaces	ice-cream seller	mettre	to put on (clothes)
		nager	to swim
l'eau profonde	deep water	se noyer	to drown
s'amuser bien	to enjoy yourself	ôter	to take off (clothes)
crier au secours	to shout for help	sauver	to rescue
s'ennuyer	to get bored		

20 La campagne

1 J'ai toujours été frappé par la variété des paysages **en France**.

1 I've always been struck by the variety of scenery **in France**.

2 Des **lacs**, des montagnes, des cascades, des **forêts**, des prairies – on y **trouve** tout.

2 **Lakes**, mountains, waterfalls, **forests**, meadows – everything is **found** there.

3 Les citadins prennent beaucoup de plaisir à faire des sorties à la **campagne**.

3 City dwellers get a lot of pleasure from going on trips to the **countryside**.

4 A **la montagne** des belvédères offrent des panoramas magnifiques.

4 In **the mountains** vantage points offer magnificent views.

5 Les petits hameaux perdus en pleine campagne sont tout à fait charmants.

5 Little villages miles from anywhere in the countryside are quite charming.

6 On trouve **agréable** de **pique-niquer** à l'ombre d'un **arbre** au bord d'un ruisseau.

6 People find it **enjoyable** to **picnic** in the shade of a **tree** by the side of a stream.

7 Pourquoi est-ce toujours moi que piquent les guêpes? C'est agaçant!

7 Why is it always me that the wasps sting? It's a nuisance!

8 J'aime bavarder avec les paysans. Leurs attitudes sont beaucoup plus saines qu'en **ville**.

8 I like chatting with country people. Their attitudes are much healthier than in **town**.

9 Ils **se fâchent** – et à juste titre – quand les citadins ne respectent pas la **campagne**.

9 They **get annoyed** – and rightly so – when town people don't respect the **countryside**

10 Ils **oublient de fermer** les barrières ou laissent leurs ordures, par exemple.

10 They **forget to shut** gates, or leave their rubbish, for example.

11 J'adore voir les moutons sauter dans les prés, ce qui nous fait **penser au printemps**.

11 I love to see the sheep skipping about in the meadows, which makes us **think of spring**.

12 En **automne** la campagne est triste mais pittoresque.

12 In **autumn** the countryside is sad but picturesque.

A Translate into French

1 The family went on a trip to the countryside.   2 They decided to picnic at the side of the road.   3 I adore forests and lakes.   4 The wasp had just stung him.   5 They used to chat with some country people.   6 The farmer got angry because they had left the gate open.
7 The bull chased the two young boys.   8 A path crossed the meadow.

B Complétez la phrase

1 Les citadins peu respectueux vont à la campagne et laissent —.
   (a) *leurs ordres*
   (b) *leurs odeurs*
   (c) *leurs ordures*

2 L'extrême beauté du paysage automnal était — incroyable.
   (a) *un peu*
   (b) *assez*
   (c) *tout à fait*

3 A cause du temps ensoleillé on a mangé —.
   (a) *avant l'aube*
   (b) *de l'ambre solaire*
   (c) *à l'ombre*

4 C'est un village isolé? – Bien sûr, c'est tout à fait —.
   (a) *hors de vue*
   (b) *varié*
   (c) *perdu*

C Questions orales

1 Pourquoi les citadins aiment-ils passer le dimanche à la campagne?
2 Quels genres de paysage aimez-vous? Pourquoi?
3 Qu'est-ce qu'on voit à la campagne au printemps?
4 Pourquoi les citadins ne sont-ils pas toujours les bienvenus à la campagne?
5 Pourquoi est-ce que tant de jeunes gens ont quitté la campagne?
7 Racontez ce que vous avez fait la dernière fois que vous êtes sorti en famille à la campagne?

le champ	field	la ferme	farm
le chemin	path	la mare	pond
l'endroit	spot, place	la vache	cow
le fermier	farmer	poursuivre	to chase
le taureau	bull	traverser	to cross
la colline	hill	se trouver	to be situated

21 L'hôtel

1 Si vous voulez **descendre à** l'hôtel en France . . .

1 If you want **to stay at** a hotel in France . . .

2 vous avez vraiment l'embarras du choix.

2 you really are spoilt for choice.

3 Les hôtels de luxe offrent **la pension complète** à une clientèle internationale.

3 Luxury hotels offer **full board** to an international clientele.

4 Les niveaux de service et de confort sont très élevés.

4 The standards of service and comfort are very high.

5 D'autre part, les petites **pensions de famille** peuvent être très accueillantes.

5 On the other hand, the small **family guest houses** can be very welcoming.

6 Plusieurs formules se présentent : demi-pension, **chambre** avec ou sans **petit déjeuner**.

6 Several options are available : half-board, **room** with or without **breakfast**.

7 Le **syndicat d'initiative** peut vous renseigner et vous **aider à choisir** votre logement.

7 The **local tourist office** is able to give you information and **help you choose** your accommodation.

8 La liste officielle précise pour chaque établissement les différentes facilités . . .

8 The official list specifies the different facilities for each establishment . . .

9 **ascenseurs**, service de blanchisserie, restauration.

9 **lifts**, laundry service, catering facilities.

10 En arrivant, vous devez vous adresser à la réception pour remplir votre fiche de voyageur.

10 When you arrive, you have to go to the reception desk to fill in your registration form.

11 Un grand **hôtel** devrait être **fier** de sa cuisine et de sa **cave**.

11 A large **hotel** should be **proud** of its cooking and its wine **cellar**.

12 Le maître d'hôtel et son personnel sont toujours à votre service.

12 The head waiter and his staff are always at your service.

l'employé	employee	régler la facture	pay the bill
le pourboire	tip	réserver à l'avance	book in advance
le propriétaire	owner	se renseigner	to enquire
la chambre	room	à un/deux lit(s)	with one/two bed(s)
la douche	shower	complet	full

A Translate into French

1 They stopped at a hotel that night.   2 We took a twin-bedded room.
3 He took a shower in his private bathroom.   4 We made enquiries at
the local tourist information office.   5 She went down in the lift.
6 Mr Lorne settled the bill and left.   7 The owner said we hadn't
booked the room in advance.   8 That hotel was full; we had to find
another that evening.   9 We gave the chamber maid a tip.

B Compréhension

L'été dernier nous avons passé trois semaines en France, descendant
dans toute une variété d'hôtels et de pensions. La formule variait selon
nos moyens financiers – il nous restait de moins en moins d'argent à
mesure que s'approchait la fin du séjour. Tout franchement je préfère
l'ambiance de la petite pension, avec un propriétaire serviable mais
accueillant, au grand hôtel tout confort où il manque quand même
quelque chose. J'ai toujours l'impression – sans doute fausse – que le
personnel dans ces établissements bien prestigieux vous regarde comme
si vous alliez partir sans régler votre facture.

1 (a) Le choix de l'établissement dépendait de l'argent qui restait.
  (b) Les mesures financières n'étaient pas variables.
  (c) Le narrateur recevait une petite pension.
  (d) Les hôtels devenaient de plus en plus prestigieux au cours du
        séjour.
2 (a) Pour le narrateur le petit hôtel a plus de caractère.
  (b) Le narrateur trouve que le service au grand hôtel est excellent.
  (c) Le narrateur aime surtout la propriété de la petite pension.
  (d) Le narrateur trouve que le confort manque dans le grand hôtel.
3 (a) Au grand hôtel on croit sans doute que vous allez partir sans
        payer.
  (b) Au grand hôtel on semble vous regarder d'un air méfiant.
  (c) Le narrateur s'est empressé de partir sans régler sa facture.
  (d) Le narrateur a une bonne impression du personnel au grand
        hôtel.

C Questions orales

1 Décrivez ce qu'on fait en arrivant dans un hôtel en France.
2 Comment un syndicat d'initiative peut-il vous être utile?
3 Préféreriez-vous faire un séjour dans un grand hôtel de luxe ou dans
  une petite pension de famille? Pourquoi?

la femme de chambre	chambermaid
la salle de bain privée	private bathroom

22 Le temps

1 Je **viens de voir** la prévision de météo à la télé après le **journal** de huit heures.

2 'Dans le nord il fera frais avec des rafales de **vent** et des **averses de pluie**.

3 Dans le Midi il fera plus doux avec des éclaircies.'

4 A Noël il gèle très souvent. Les piétons doivent faire attention aux trottoirs verglassés.

5 L'**automne** dernier il a fait un temps tout à fait incroyable.

6 Le jour de mon départ en vacances le **soleil** brillait et il n'y avait pas un seul nuage au ciel.

7 Pâques dernier, par contre, **il a fait un temps maussade** et peu chaud.

8 **Au printemps** l'herbe commence à pousser et tout fleurit.

9 **En hiver** le verglas et le brouillard sont très hasardeux pour l'automobiliste.

10 **En été** des orages éclatent de temps en temps avec du tonnerre et des éclairs.

11 Le temps hivernal a son côté positif pour ceux qui **font du ski** ou du patinage.

12 Des **chutes** abondantes **de neige** provoquent des problèmes au moment du redoux.

1 I've **just seen** the weather forecast on the telly after the eight o'clock **news**.

2 'In the north it will be cool with gusts of **wind** and **showers**.

3 In the South of France it will be warmer with bright intervals.'

4 At Christmas it very often freezes. Pedestrians have to be careful of slippery pavements.

5 Last **autumn** the weather was quite incredible.

6 The day I went on holiday the **sun** was shining and there wasn't a single cloud in the sky.

7 Last Easter, on the other hand, **it was gloomy** and not at all warm.

8 **In the spring** the grass begins to grow and everything blossoms.

9 **In winter** black ice and fog are very dangerous for the motorist.

10 **In summer** storms break out from time to time with thunder and lightning.

11 The winter weather has its positive side for people **who go skiing** or skating.

12 Heavy **snowfalls** cause problems at the time of the thaw.

est/ouest/sud   east/west/south

faire beau   to be nice (weather)

A Translate into French

1 The day they left for their holidays it was foggy.   **2** It's freezing in December.   **3** Last summer the weather was beautiful.   **4** When we arrived it was windy and raining.   **5** You need to carry an umbrella when the weather is bad.

B Complétez la phrase

1 Il — quand il fait –10 degrés centigrade.
2 La saison où les plantes fleurissent s'appelle le —.
3 La prévision de météo annonce le — qu'il fera.
4 En novembre le — rend difficile la vue au volant.

C Qu'est-ce qu'on répondrait?

1 Il fait peu chaud.
   (a) *Oui, il fait un peu chaud.*
   (b) *Oui, il fait frais.*
   (c) *Il fait vraiment chaud.*
2 Ce temps glacial a son bon côté.
   (a) *Peut-être pour les skieurs.*
   (b) *Peut-être pour les automobilistes.*
   (c) *Peut-être pour les vendeurs de glaces.*
3 Les routes sont vraiment glissantes.
   (a) *C'est vraiment incroyable en hiver.*
   (b) *C'est un hasard pour les piétons surtout.*
   (c) *Il y a probablement du verglas.*
4 Il fait doux mais il y aura certainement des averses.
   (a) *C'est vrai – il pleut mais il fera plus chaud.*
   (b) *Il faut que je prenne mon parapluie.*
   (c) *Il faut que je m'habille chaudement.*

D Questions orales

1 Quelle saison de l'année préférez-vous et pourquoi?
2 Quel temps a-t-il fait pendant les vacances de Noël/de Pâques?
3 Quel temps doit-il faire pour qu'on puisse faire du patinage?
4 Quel temps faisait-il le jour où vous êtes parti en vacances l'été dernier?
5 Pourquoi est-ce que les Anglais parlent toujours du temps?
6 Quel temps fait-il en novembre normalement?

faire du brouillard	to be foggy	faire du soleil	to be sunny
faire froid	to be cold	faire du vent	to be windy
faire mauvais	to be bad (weather)	neiger	to snow
		pleuvoir	to rain

23 L'heure

1 'Vous **écoutez** France Inter. Il est neuf heures précises.'

1 'You're **listening** to France Inter. The time now – exactly nine o'clock.'

2 A l'**horloge** de la **mairie** il est **onze heures vingt-cinq** du matin.

2 By the **town hall clock** it's **eleven twenty-five** a.m.

3 Mon réveil sonnera à **sept heures et quart demain matin**.

3 My alarm will go off at **seven-fifteen tomorrow morning**.

4 Le coup d'envoi était prévu pour **trois heures moins le quart.**

4 The kick-off was scheduled for a **quarter to three.**

5 La finale s'était disputée la veille au soir.

5 The final had been played the previous evening.

6 Je suis **arrivé en retard** parce que la **pendule** de la cuisine retardait de dix minutes.

6 I **arrived late** because the kitchen **clock** was ten minutes slow.

7 Elle s'est **couchée à minuit** après une **soirée** fatigante.

7 She **went to bed** at **midnight** after a tiring **evening**.

8 Il **s'est levé** tôt – à cinq heures et demie – et a passé toute la journée **en plein air**.

8 He **got up early** – at five-thirty – and spent the whole day in the **open air**.

9 Je te verrai **plus tard** dans la matinée – vers **midi et demi.**

9 I'll see you **later on** in the morning – around **half-past twelve.**

10 Le **journal** passe à la télé à six heures moins vingt du soir en Angleterre.

10 The **news** is on the telly at twenty to six in the evening in England.

11 Ma **nouvelle montre** à affichage numérique n'avance que de quelques secondes par semaine.

11 My **new** digital **watch** gains only a few seconds per week.

12 Mon **frère** a l'habitude de remonter **sa montre** avant de **se coucher.**

12 My **brother** is in the habit of winding up his **watch** before **going to bed.**

un après-midi	afternoon	le quart d'heure	quarter of an hour
trois heures de l'après-midi	three p.m.	le rendez-vous	appointment
		la demi-heure	half hour

A Translate into French

1 She arrived early. 2 Mr Grossetête had arrived late at his office.
3 They spent two hours listening to the radio. 4 She spent the entire
day writing letters. 5 It was exactly eight o'clock by the living-room
clock. 6 His watch was twenty minutes fast. 7 He consulted his
watch: he was on time. 8 The church clock struck eleven a.m. as he
was leaving the supermarket. 9 The alarm clock went off at six-
twenty a.m. 10 They spent an interesting morning. 11 The evening
was very tiring. 12 I finished the work a quarter of an hour ago.

B De quoi est-ce qu'on parle?

1 On la porte au poignet.
2 Elle indique l'heure sur un bâtiment public à l'extérieur.
3 On le trouve souvent dans une chambre à coucher pour indiquer
l'heure.
4 Elle indique l'heure à l'intérieur d'une maison ou d'un bâtiment.

C Qu'est-ce qu'on répondrait?

1 C'est ridicule – ma montre retarde de deux heures.
   (a) *Je suis deux heures à l'avance.*
   (b) *J'aurais dû la retarder.*
   (c) *J'ai dû oublier de la remonter.*
2 Je regrette – elle est partie il y a quinze minutes.
   (a) *Alors je suis trop tard!*
   (b) *Alors je suis plus tard!*
   (c) *Tiens – elle est partie il y a une quinzaine!*
3 Je me suis réveillé à une heure du matin.
   (a) *Tu es bien paresseux de rester au lit jusqu'à une heure.*
   (b) *Alors tu as été à l'heure.*
   (c) *Alors tu n'as pas pu dormir.*

D Questions orales

1 Racontez exactement ce que vous avez fait hier soir entre cinq
   heures et dix heures.
2 Qu'est-ce que vous faisiez à huit heures ce matin?
3 Pourquoi est-ce qu'on a besoin d'une montre?

consulter	to consult	à l'heure	on time
passer cinq minutes	to spend five minutes	il y a dix	ten minutes
à + infinitive	doing something	minutes	ago
sonner six heures	to strike six	plus tôt	earlier

24 La santé

1 La semaine **dernière** je n'étais pas dans mon assiette.

1 **Last** week I was feeling under the weather.

2 J'avais attrapé un rhume – j'avais de la fièvre, je toussais et j'éternuais.

2 I had caught a cold – I had a temperature. was coughing and sneezing.

3 J'avais non seulement **mal à la tête,** mais **mal aux oreilles** aussi.

3 I not only had a **headache,** but **earache** as well.

4 Je me suis vite rétabli et j'étais en pleine forme après quelques jours de repos.

4 I soon recovered and was feeling fit after a few days rest.

5 Notre **famille** est prédisposée aux accidents en ce moment.

5 Our **family** is accident-prone at the moment.

6 Mon **frère** s'est blessé **la jambe** en jouant au volleyball.

6 My **brother** hurt **his leg** playing volleyball.

7 Mon **père** s'est coupé la main en **réparant** la voiture.

7 My **father** cut his hand **repairing** the car.

8 Ma **mère** lui a mis un pansement et un sparadrap.

8 My **mother** put on a dressing and a sticking plaster for him.

9 Les visiteurs en France qui sont gourmands risquent très souvent d'avoir mal au ventre ou du moins une indigestion.

9 Visitors to France who are greedy frequently risk having stomach-ache or at least indigestion.

10 Si je prends un **petit déjeuner** copieux avant un **voyage** en voiture, j'ai souvent mal au cœur.

10 If I have a big **breakfast** before a car **journey** I often feel sick.

11 Je dois avouer que je n'**aime** pas du tout l'ambiance . . .

11 I must confess that I don't **like** at all the atmosphere . . .

12 des **salles d'attente** et des cabinets de consultation.

12 of **waiting rooms** and surgeries.

un comprimé d'aspirine	aspirin tablet	la blessure	injury
le médecin	doctor	l'infirmière	nurse
le/la malade	patient	faire venir	to send for
le médicament	medicine	se guérir	to get better
le sang	blood	se sentir malade	to feel ill
		tomber malade	to fall ill

A Translate into French

1 He had hurt his arm. 2 He cut his finger. 3 My ears are hurting.
4 Her head ached. 5 I've just caught a cold and I'm running a
temperature. 6 He recovered three days later. 7 He felt sick after
the meal. 8 My mother fell ill. 9 They were seriously injured in the
accident. 10 His injuries were serious.

B Compréhension

Les salles d'attente et les cabinets de consultations sont bondés de gens
qui gaspillent très souvent le temps des médecins, dont la patience et les
forces sont limitées. Ceux qui sont enrhumés, par exemple, feraient
bien de garder le lit et d'avaler quelques comprimés d'aspirine au lieu
de consulter un médecin déjà surchargé de travail. Il y a quand même
des circonstances où il est prudent de passer voir le médecin – s'il y a
la possibilité que du sol infecte une coupure, une piqûre s'impose avant
de mettre un pansement.

1 (a) On paie cher les services d'un médecin.
   (b) Les médecins ne sont pas surhumains.
   (c) Les médecins gaspillent leur temps normalement.
   (d) Le nombre de malades est limité malheureusement.
2 (a) Certains malades pourraient se guérir chez eux.
   (b) Certains malades font bon de garder le lit avec leur rhume.
   (c) Certains malades sont surchargés de travail.
   (d) Certains malades sont allés aux lieux de consultation.
3 (a) Si vous vous coupez dans le jardin, vous ferez bien de voir le
       médecin.
   (b) Si vous descendez dans le sous-sol, allez voir le médecin.
   (c) Si une guêpe vous pique, allez tout de suite au cabinet.
   (d) Avant de mettre un pansement vous êtes obligé de voir le
       médecin.

C Questions orales

1 Quels sont les symptômes d'un rhume?
2 Qu'est-ce que vous faites si vous avez attrapé un rhume?
3 Qu'est-ce qui arrive si vous mangez trop de pommes?
4 Qu'est-ce que vous feriez si vous vous coupiez le bras?
5 Dans quelles circonstances est-ce qu'on a mal au cœur normalement?

aveugle	blind	muet	dumb
blessé	injured	sourd	deaf
grave(ment)	serious(ly)	ça va mieux?	feeling better?

25 Le corps

1 Nous sommes beaucoup plus conscients actuellement de l'importance de l'exercice physique.

1 We're much more aware nowadays of the importance of physical exercise.

2 Le footing est avantageux pour les poumons et le **cœur**.

2 Jogging is beneficial to the lungs and **heart**.

3 La natation exerce des muscles aux **jambes**, aux **genoux**, aux **bras** et aux **épaules**.

3 Swimming exercises muscles in the **legs**, **knees**, **arms** and **shoulders**.

4 Est-ce que je me fais du bien en faisant de la planche à roulettes?

4 Am I doing myself any good going skateboarding?

5 Si vous ne voulez pas prendre des kilos, évitez les sucreries et les pâtisseries dans votre régime!

5 If you don't want to put on weight, avoid sweet things and pastries in your diet!

6 Les **fruits** sont très bons pour la peau, les **yeux** et les **cheveux**.

6 **Fruit** is very good for the skin, **eyes** and **hair**.

7 Voilà pourquoi nous gardons l'image de la jeune paysanne . . .

7 That's why we retain the image of the young country-girl . . .

8 à la **figure** fraîche, aux lèvres **rouges** et aux joues roses.

8 with a fresh **complexion**, **red** lips and rosy cheeks.

9 Il ne faut pas négliger l'entretien du corps si on veut **rester** en bonne santé.

9 You musn't neglect body maintenance, if you want to **remain** in good health.

10 On doit se couper les ongles et se faire couper **les cheveux**, par exemple.

10 You must cut your nails and get your **hair** cut for instance.

11 Certains ne trouvent pas impossible de garder leur ligne jusqu'à un bel âge.

11 Some people don't find it impossible to keep in trim to a ripe old age.

12 Malgré quelques rides et la **tête chauve**, ils se portent comme le Pont-Neuf!

12 Despite a few wrinkles and a **bald head,** they are as fit as fiddles!

un œil	eye	la main	hand
le visage	face	une oreille	ear
la bouche	mouth	gros (grosse)	fat
la dent	tooth	mince	thin

A Translate into English

A l'heure actuelle des milliers de gens commencent à se rendre compte que l'exercice physique non seulement vous maintient en forme mais aussi peut enrichir votre manière de vie. Les bienfaits physiques ne sont pas à nier et touchent toute une série d'organes et de muscles du corps – poumons, cœur, jambes, genoux, dos, bras – mais ceux qui se passionnent pour le footing, par exemple, parlent aussi d'une tranquillité intérieure qui est très thérapeutique, surtout pour l'homme d'affaires qui souffre de tension nerveuse. Le régime joue aussi son rôle, tout aussi important que celui de l'exercice. Pour garder sa ligne on n'est pas obligé de suivre un régime exotique mais plutôt de réduire sa consommation de sucreries. On a tout intérêt à cultiver de telles habitudes et attitudes dans sa jeunesse si on veut vivre à un âge avancé. Une belle ligne et une manière de vie toujours active ne sont pas hors de question même quand on aura dépassé la soixantaine.

B Qu'est-ce qu'on répondrait?

1 Michel vient de se faire couper les cheveux.
   (a) *Qu'il est beau!*
   (b) *Il devra aller au coiffeur.*
   (c) *Il s'est coupé les cheveux lui-même.*

2 Qu'est-ce que tu ferais à ma place pour perdre des kilos?
   (a) *J'ai pris des kilos.*
   (b) *Je mangerais moins.*
   (c) *Je mangeais moins à ta place.*

3 Elle a une belle figure.
   (a) *Elle ne mange presque rien.*
   (b) *Elle ne pèse que 40 kilos.*
   (c) *Sa peau est exquise.*

4 Son visage est creusé de rides, n'est-ce pas?
   (a) *Oui, mais autrement il se porte bien, vu son âge.*
   (b) *Oui, il a la peau belle.*
   (c) *Je n'aime pas ses rideaux.*

C Questions orales

1 A quoi servent les yeux?
2 Pourquoi va-t-on chez le coiffeur/au salon de coiffure?
3 A quoi reconnaît-on qu'un homme est très âgé?
4 Dans quel sens est-ce que l'exercice est salutaire?
5 Qu'est-ce que vous faites pour vous maintenir en forme?
6 Qu'est-ce qu'on doit faire pour garder sa ligne?

26 Les vêtements

1 Depuis plusieurs années les commerçants de la côte sud de l'Angleterre . . .

2 se trouvent pris à l'assaut par des acheteurs français.

3 Dans les grands **magasins** les **vêtements** de confection se vendent en grosses quantités.

4 Dans les rayons homme on **trouve** souvent des Françaises qui achètent une **veste** ou **un pantalon** pour leur **mari**.

5 Les chemisettes, les **jupes**, les **manteaux** et les **chaussures** sont très demandés.

6 Les **prix** des tricots et des produits de laine sont très avantageux.

7 Le prêt à porter anglais a gagné une bonne image de marque.

8 L'homme d'affaires **habillé** en **complet** rayé et coiffé d'un **chapeau** melon . . .

9 a été remplacé par un **jeune homme** en tenue plus décontractée de jean et bras de chemise.

10 A Noël les acheteurs d'outre Manche feraient bien d'apporter un imper . . .

11 et de **mettre** leur pardessus et leurs **gants** avant d'embarquer sur le ferry!

12 On se demande quelle est l'attitude des douanes françaises envers ces affaires fantastiques.

1 For several years shopkeepers on the south coast of England . . .

2 have been finding themselves invaded by French shoppers.

3 In the big **stores** ready-to-wear **clothes** are sold in huge quantities.

4 In the men's departments you often **find** Frenchwomen buying a **jacket** or **a pair of trousers** for their **husband**.

5 Blouses, **skirts**, **top-coats** and **shoes** are very much in demand.

6 The **prices** of sweaters and woollen products are very attractive.

7 British off-the-peg clothes have acquired a good brand image.

8 The businessman **dressed** in a pinstripe **suit** and wearing a bowler **hat** . . .

9 has been replaced by a **young man** in more relaxed dress of jeans and shirtsleeves.

10 At Christmas shoppers from across the Channel would do well to bring a mac . . .

11 and to **put on** their overcoat and **gloves** before getting on the ferry!

12 One wonders what the attitude of French customs is to all these fantastic bargains.

| le collant | tights | la culotte | shorts |
| la chaussette | sock | la manche | sleeve |

A Translate into French

1 He was wearing a green jacket and blue trousers. 2 She tried on the sweater but it didn't suit her. 3 She wore a white skirt.

B De quoi est-ce qu'on parle?

1 On le porte sur la tête.
2 On le porte quand il pleut si on n'a pas de parapluie.
3 C'est l'équivalent pour la femme de la chemise.
4 On les porte pour protéger les mains contre le froid.
5 C'est un produit de laine qui a été tricoté.

C Qu'est-ce qu'on répondrait?

1 Pardon, monsieur, pour le rayon homme s'il vous plaît?
   (a) *Quel homme, madame?*
   (b) *Oui, il y a des hommes dans ce rayon.*
   (c) *En face de vous, madame.*
2 Il y a des affaires fantastiques dans ce magasin.
   (a) *Oui, c'est une fantaisie.*
   (b) *C'est pour cela qu'ils sont pris d'assaut.*
   (c) *C'est vrai, les prix ne sont pas tellement avantageux.*
3 Les tricots sont très demandés aujourd'hui.
   (a) *Je leur ai déjà demandé.*
   (b) *Je me demande pourquoi quand il fait si froid.*
   (c) *Cela ne m'étonne pas, vu la température.*
4 Il n'a pas l'air très décontracté, il faut bien le dire.
   (a) *Il faudrait porter un complet et un chapeau melon.*
   (b) *Il aurait dû mettre son jean pour être plus à l'aise.*
   (c) *Cela ne m'étonne pas quand il est en bras de chemise.*

D Questions orales

1 Qu'est-ce que vous mettez pour sortir quand il pleut?
2 Quelle est la différence entre ce que vous portez en hiver et en été?
3 Qu'avez-vous fait la dernière fois que vous avez acheté des chaussures?
4 Décrivez ce que vous portez aujourd'hui.
5 Qu'est-ce que vous portiez quand vous étiez à l'école primaire?
6 Décrivez la tenue de votre équipe de football/de hockey.

le parapluie	umbrella	la taille	size
essayer	to try (on)	gris clair	light grey
vert foncé	dark green	'cela lui va bien'	'that suits her'

27 Les animaux

1 Pendant les vacances de Pâques on a **visité** une réserve.

2 Les singes ont **grimpé** sur le **toit** de la voiture d'une manière insolente.

3 Un des gardiens était en train de **donner à manger** aux lions.

4 Ce sont des **bêtes** féroces et dangereuses mais d'une beauté fascinante.

5 Je **me demandais** comment les girafes s'adaptaient à notre climat bien différent.

6 Je préfère **voir** les animaux sauvages dans un environnement plus ou moins naturel.

7 Les ours, par exemple, ont l'air bien triste quand ils sont enfermés dans une cage.

8 Je dois l'avouer : j'ai horreur des serpents, des souris et des araignées.

9 Nous avons trois animaux chez nous – un **chien**, une perruche et un **poisson rouge**.

10 Je **tiens** notre **chien** en laisse quand je **le promène** dans le **parc**.

11 Nos **voisins** nourrissent les animaux quand nous ne sommes pas là.

12 Il est très **important** de bien soigner les animaux.

1 During the Easter holidays we **visited** a safari park.

2 The monkeys cheekily **climbed** on the **roof** of our car.

3 One of the wardens was right in the middle **of feeding** the lions.

4 They are wild and dangerous **animals** but with a fascinating beauty.

5 I **was wondering** how the giraffes adapted to our climate which is so different.

6 I prefer to **see** wild animals in a more or less natural setting.

7 Bears, for example, look very sad when they're locked up in a cage.

8 I have to admit it : I'm scared to death of snakes, mice and spiders.

9 We have three pets at home – a **dog,** a budgie and a **goldfish**.

10 I **keep** our **dog** on a lead when I **take him for a walk** in the **park**.

11 Our **neighbours** feed the pets when we're away.

12 It's very **important** to look after pets properly.

le cirque	circus	le lapin	rabbit
le chasseur	hunter	la tortue	tortoise
le fusil	rifle	avoir peur de	to be scared of

A Translate into French

1 He was taking the dog for a walk when the accident happened.
2 She was scared of mice. 3 The dog ran out into the street. 4 The lions escaped from the cage. 5 The hunters had to shoot at the savage animal. 6 The bear had just escaped from the circus.

B Translate into English

Les enfants, lorsqu'ils ont aperçu l'ours, sont restés immobiles. Ils n'ont même pas eu l'idée de se sauver. L'ours s'était avancé en les regardant. Ses yeux brillaient. Puis il a détourné la tête. Jérôme venait de s'avancer. Peut-être avait-il tellement peur qu'il ne savait plus ce qu'il faisait. Il s'est arrêté à quelques pas de l'ours qui se dressait sur ses pattes de derrière. (ox)

C Qu'est-ce qu'on répondrait?

1 Les lions ont l'air bien content, papa.
   (a) *Oui, on vient de les manger.*
   (b) *Oui, ils viennent de se manger.*
   (c) *Oui, on vient de leur donner à manger.*
2 Puis-je promener le chien, maman?
   (a) *Oui, on peut te promener.*
   (b) *Oui, mais n'oublie pas sa laisse.*
   (c) *Oui, tu peux le laisser.*
3 Regarde! Ils sont en train de s'évader.
   (a) *Il faut faire venir le gardien!*
   (b) *C'est une cage bien enfermée!*
   (c) *Il faut arrêter le train.*
4 Que ferait-on si cette bête s'évadait?
   (a) *On s'évadait.*
   (b) *Il faudrait se sauver le plus vite possible.*
   (c) *On l'a enfermée dans sa cage le plus vite possible.*

D Questions orales

1 Est-ce que vous avez des animaux chez vous? Décrivez-les.
2 Pourquoi est-il important de garder un chien en laisse en ville?
3 Faites la description d'une visite que vous avez faite à une réserve ou à un jardin zoologique.
4 Est-ce que vous avez peur de certains animaux?

s'évader de	to escape from	se sauver	to run away
faire la chasse à	to hunt	tirer sur	to shoot at
poursuivre	to chase		

28 Quelques pays

1 J'ai toujours eu l'ambition de faire le tour du **monde**.

1 I've always had the ambition to go round the **world**.

2 J'adore les pays ensoleillés au climat doux – l'Italie, l'Espagne, le Portugal.

2 I love sunny countries with a mild climate – Italy, Spain, Portugal.

3 En Suisse on **parle** français, allemand, italien ou romanche selon la région.

3 In Switzerland they **speak** French, German, Italian or Romansh, according to the area.

4 Le **coût de la vie** est cher pour les touristes, car le franc suisse est une monnaie forte.

4 The **cost of living** is expensive for tourists because the Swiss franc is a strong currency.

5 La **capitale** de la Belgique, Bruxelles, est de grand intérêt historique.

5 The **capital** of Belgium, Brussels, is of considerable historical interest.

6 J'ai un copain qui a fait une croisière sur le Rhin, **fleuve** de grande importance.

6 I have a friend who's been on a cruise on the Rhine, a **river** of considerable size.

7 L'Afrique est un continent où beaucoup de **pays** sont toujours en train de se développer.

7 Africa is a continent where many **countries** are still in the process of developing.

8 Le Moyen Orient présente un grand nombre de problèmes sur le plan international.

8 The Middle East presents a large number of problems on an international level.

9 La Chine est un pays mystérieux pour la plupart des Européens.

9 China is a mysterious country for the majority of Europeans.

10 Le Japon a un style de vie qui est plus occidental.

10 Japan has a life style which is more western.

11 Je m'intéresse à l'art et à la sculpture – voilà pourquoi je voudrais **visiter** la Grèce.

11 I am interested in art and sculpture – that's why I would like to **visit** Greece.

12 Les États-Unis et le Canada deviennent de plus en plus accessibles.

12 The USA and Canada are becoming more and more accessible.

l'Allemagne (f.)	Germany	la Russie	Russia
la Grande Bretagne	Great Britain	anglais	English

A De quel pays est-ce qu'on parle?
1 Pays ensoleillé où les touristes assistent aux courses de taureaux.
2 Groupe de quatre pays – l'Angleterre, l'Écosse, le Pays de Galles et l'Irlande du Nord.
3 Pays européen où on parle quatre langues, dont trois sont majeures et une mineure.
4 Pays d'Europe occidental où on parle deux langues, le français et le flamand.
5 Pays oriental qui a été beaucoup influencé par la sociéte occidentale.
6 Pays du Nouveau Monde dont plusieurs provinces sont francophiles.
7 La Place Rouge est au centre de sa capitale.
8 Groupe d'une cinquantaine d'états dont la capitale est Washington sur la côte ouest.

B Qu'est-ce qu'on répondrait?
1 C'est la première fois que je fais un voyage aux États-Unis.
   (a) *Vous vous êtes bien amusé la première fois.*
   (b) *Moi aussi, je l'ai visité plusieurs fois.*
   (c) *Tout sera nouveau pour vous.*
2 Comment as-tu trouvé le coût de la vie en Suède?
   (a) *Ce n'est pas tellement accessible du point de vue financier.*
   (b) *Je l'ai trouvé au bout de trois semaines.*
   (c) *On y achète beaucoup d'eau de vie.*
3 Tu n'as jamais été en Chine?
   (a) *Non, je n'y suis jamais allé.*
   (b) *Non, il n'y a pas d'été en Chine.*
   (c) *Non, mais j'aimerais voir l'Occident.*

C Questions orales
1 Aimeriez-vous faire une croisière cet hiver? Pourquoi/pas?
2 Pourquoi la France est-elle un pays favorable à la culture de la vigne?
3 Quels pays avez-vous visités? Quelles étaient vos impressions de ces pays?
4 Pourquoi est-ce que certains pays deviennent plus accessibles?
5 Quels pays aimeriez-vous visiter surtout? Pourquoi?
6 Est-ce que vous étudiez d'autres langues étrangères, à part le français?

---

espagnol	Spanish
russe	Russian
l'Anglais; l'Espagnol; le Russe	Englishman, Spaniard, Russian

29 Le crime ne paie pas

1 **Samedi dernier** je me **suis réveillé** à **deux heures du matin**.

2 J'étais convaincu que j'avais **entendu** un **bruit** qui **venait** d'en bas.

3 Sur la pointe des pieds je suis **allé** dans la **chambre** de mes parents.

4 'Il y a **quelqu'un** en bas,' leur ai-je expliqué à voix basse.

5 Mon **père** ne tenait pas beaucoup à descendre pour saisir l'intrus.

6 **La veille au soir** deux cambrioleurs **étaient entrés par effraction** dans la maison de nos voisins.

7 On avait **volé** quelques bijoux, un chéquier et 500 francs en espèces après avoir forcé un petit coffre-fort.

8 Mon **père a décidé** de **téléphoner** à la police, composant le numéro avec le minimum de bruit.

9 Les agents sont **arrivés** au bout de quelques **minutes**.

10 L'intrus était sur le point de **sortir** par une **fenêtre** entrouverte.

11 Il s'est sauvé et les **agents** l'ont poursuivi à fond de train.

12 Il n'a pas pu s'évader. On l'a emmené au **commissariat**, les menottes aux poignets.

1 **Last Saturday** I **woke up** at **two a.m.**

2 I was convinced I had **heard** a **noise coming** from downstairs.

3 On tiptoe I **went** into my parents' **bedroom**.

4 'There's **someone** downstairs,' I explained to them in a low voice.

5 My **father** wasn't very keen on going downstairs to tackle the intruder.

6 The **previous evening** two burglars **had broken into** our neighbours' house.

7 They had **stolen** some jewellery, a cheque book and 500 francs in cash after breaking into a small safe.

8 My **father decided** to **telephone** the police, dialling the number with as little noise as possible.

9 The police **arrived** within a few **minutes**.

10 The intruder was about to **leave** through a half open **window**.

11 He ran off and the **policemen** chased him at high speed.

12 He didn't manage to get away. He was taken, handcuffed, to the **police station**.

un inconnu	stranger	avoir peur	to be frightened
le revolver	gun	menacer	to threaten
le témoin	witness	tenir	to hold

A Translate into French
1 They heard a noise coming from downstairs. **2** The thieves ran away. **3** The burglars were taken to the police station. **4** I phoned the police. **5** They had stolen a car.

B Translate into English
Un jour j'étais assis à la terrasse d'un café, profitant de ces quelques moments de repos pour jeter un coup d'œil sur mon journal. A la première page il y avait un article sur une entrée par effraction dans une pharmacie du quartier. Une grosse quantité de stupéfiants avait disparu. Les détails du vol étaient suivis d'un signalement de deux hommes que recherchait la police. Je venais de poser mon journal sur la table et j'étais sur le point de prendre mon café quand j'ai remarqué un type sinistre à la table voisine. J'ai repris mon journal et relu le signalement: c'était bien un des malfaiteurs, j'en étais convaincu. Après avoir réglé mon addition, j'ai pénétré dans le café pour trouver une cabine téléphonique. Une voiture de police est arrivée à toute vitesse et trois agents en sont descendus, des revolvers à la main. Le criminel s'est rendu avec le minimum de résistance sans essayer de s'évader. Les agents ont été bien contents d'avoir arrêté ce malfaiteur. En quelques jours ils avaient trouvé le complice et récupéré les stupéfiants volés. Et moi? J'ai reçu une récompense du pharmacien pour avoir reconnu ce type sinistre d'après le signalement dans le journal.

C Complétez la phrase
1 L'homme s'est sauvé mais j'ai décidé de le —.
2 J'ai vu un type menaçant qui — un revolver à la main.
3 J'ai — le criminel d'après sa photo dans le journal.
4 Les agents ne lui avaient pas passé de menottes. Il a donc pu s' —.
5 Nous habitons 32 rue Voltaire. Nos — habitent 34.
6 Mon père est descendu pour voir s'il y avait quelqu'un — —.

D Questions orales
1 Qu'est-ce que vous feriez si vous entendiez un bruit dans votre salon à quatre heures du matin?
2 A qui est-ce qu'il faut téléphoner si un crime vient d'avoir lieu?
3 Imaginez que vous avez été témoin d'un vol dans une banque. Décrivez ce qui s'est passé et donnez un signalement des malfaiteurs.

sinistre	sinister	donner un	to give a description
à toute vitesse	at high speed	signalement	
le voleur	thief	une récompense	reward
		reconnaître	to recognize

3 Getting ready for the examination

In this chapter we examine the different types of questions (*translation from French, prose composition, comprehension* (reading and listening), *essay writing, oral tests, dictation*) which may feature in your French examination. However, before tackling this chapter you should know which syllabus you are taking and for which Board: if you are not clear in your mind about this, check with your teacher. As the emphasis placed on the various questions set by the different Boards varies considerably, it is essential for you to find out:

* which type of questions you will be expected to answer
* how much time is allowed
* how many marks are allocated to each question

Once you have this information, you can then concentrate on the appropriate sections in this chapter for the syllabus of the examination you are sitting.

As a general rule, remember always to read any instructions you are given in the examination both *slowly and carefully*. Remember also the importance of *timing*. In all your revision work you should teach yourself to read the questions carefully, complete all questions to the specified length and in the time allocated whilst allowing yourself sufficient time for a rough copy and, of course, for checking through your work. If you train yourself in this way, you will be able to complete all the questions in the time allowed in the examination. You will also find that timing your revision work is a great help towards accuracy in the examination.

Translation from French

General advice

1 Read the French text all the way through at least three times.
2 Don't panic if there are words you don't know. You may be able to guess the meaning later from the context.
3 The text should make sense and should bear some relation to the title. If you have one sentence, or even one word, that seems wildly out of context with the rest of the text, you have very likely made a mistake.
4 When you check over your polished version it should read as a piece of natural English which would make good sense to someone who had never read the French text. If it sounds like a Frenchman talking charming, but broken English, there is room for improvement. Reading your answer to yourself (not out loud in the examination!) in that sort of faulty English accent may help you to spot strange English usage.
5 Practise working on timed passages as much as possible in class and at home. Pace yourself to allow time for a rough copy first. If you don't finish the passage in time, you risk losing a lot of marks, however brilliant the portion that you do complete.
6 Marks are also thrown away by missing out odd words, phrases or even whole lines. Check your translation word by word, line by line against the French. If you have missed out any words there has to be a good reason for it. Examiners know the passage well and will spot any omissions.

Frequent points of difficulty

Don't be depressed by the long list. Being aware of some of the traps should make you less likely to fall into them! Notice how vocabulary is mentioned only once, showing that translation is much more than a word test. Study a couple of points at a time, then try the test sentences beginning on p110 These are on specific points corresponding to the letters **A, B, C, D** etc. After the test sentences there is an extract from a past O level paper for you to look at.

A Tenses

Verb mistakes can cost you a lot of marks. Translating *il jouera* as *he would sing* counts as two errors (wrong meaning of verb and wrong tense; it should be *he will play*). Take careful note as follows:

1 Be sure you can recognize the past historic (see p21 and verb tables on pp183–7). Translate with a simple past in English, i.e. *he saw*, *he wrote* not *he has seen*, *he has written*.

2 Make sure you translate the imperfect in the most natural way for the particular sentence, e.g. *il voyait* could be *he saw*, *he used to see* or *he was seeing*.

3 Translate the perfect in the most natural way too, depending on the sentence. *Il a vu* could be *he saw* or *he has seen*.

4 The present tense also offers different possibilities of translation. *Je travaille* could be *I work* or *I do work* or *I am working* (see also note 6).

5 Look out for *venir de + infinitive*
je *viens* (present tense) d'arriver   I *have* just arrived
ils *venaient* (imperfect) de partir they *had* just left

6 Look out for *depuis + a time expression*.
Il enseigne (present tense) depuis dix ans.
  He *has been teaching* for ten years.
Nous essayions (imperfect) de démarrer la voiture depuis dix minutes quand . . .
  We *had been trying* to start the car for ten minutes when . . .
Note Voilà que + a time expression can be used in the same way as *depuis* above.
Voilà dix ans qu'il enseigne (present).
  He *has been teaching* for ten years.
Voilà dix minutes que nous essayions (imperfect) de démarrer la voiture.
  We *had been trying* to start the car for ten minutes.

7 Avoid translating *après avoir* and *après être* phrases word for word, e.g. *après avoir mangé* – use *after he had eaten* rather than *after having eaten*.

8 French uses the future in a more exact way than English, so don't translate word for word if the end result is strange English.
Qu'est-ce que tu *feras* quand tu *seras grand*?
  What *will you do* when you *are grown up*? (French says 'when you will be grown up'.)
Je *te donnerai* un coup de fil quand j'*aurai fini* mon travail.
  I'*ll give you* a ring when I'*ve finished* my work. (French says, 'when I will have finished my work'.)

B Verb ending -ant

1 Look out for the verb ending -*ant* which corresponds to -*ing* in English (playing, singing etc) when combined with *en* + *a verb of movement*. Note how this can be best translated.

Il est descendu en courant.

He ran down (word for word 'he went down running').

Il est sorti en se dépêchant.

He hurried out (word for word 'he went out hurrying').

2 If there is no movement, *while* would be better.

Il travaillait en chantant.

He was singing while he worked.

C Reflexives

1 Beware reflexives! Very rarely do you translate the reflexive word if you want the English to sound natural.

| il s'est réveillé | he woke up |
| je me suis coupé la main | I cut my hand |

2 Reflexive *verbs of thought* translate reasonably into English with a reflexive.

| il s'est demandé | he asked himself (he wondered) |
| je me suis dit | I said to myself |

3 Note how the reflexive is translated in these sentences.

La porte s'est ouverte.	The door opened (was opened).
Son anxiété se voyait.	His anxiety could be seen.
Le fromage se vend ici.	Cheese is sold here.
Cela ne se dit pas.	That is not said.

D On

On should only ever be translated as *one* in English if there is no better alternative. In a conversational passage translate *on* as *we*, but note some of the possibilities below.

on parle français	they speak French (French is spoken)
on a fini le travail à huit heures	the work was finished at eight o'clock
on lui a dit	he was told
on lui a demandé	he was asked
on a tué le renard	the fox was killed
On va au cinéma?	Shall we go to the cinema?

E Infinitives

1 If the infinitive links with another verb in the sentence, join them in a way that sounds natural in English.

il a réussi à gagner   he succeeded *in* winning; he managed *to* win

il a commencé par rire   he began *by* laughing

elle a refusé de partir   she refused *to* leave

2 Remember to use the participle in English when the infinitive is linked with a verb of perception (*hearing, seeing, noticing*).

Je *la voyais sortir* de la maison à sept heures.   I *used to see her leaving* the house at seven o'clock.

Je *l'ai entendu chanter*.   I *heard him singing*.

3 When a sentence begins with an infinitive, use a participle in English.

passer deux heures en métro n'est pas très agréable   *spending* two hours in the tube isn't very pleasant

4 *Au lieu de* + *infinitive, sans* + *infinitive* should be translated in English by a participle.

au lieu de travailler   instead of work*ing*

sans parler   without speak*ing*

F Word order

There are three main instances when you should change the word order in your translation.

1 After *direct speech marks*

'Félicitations!' s'est-il exclamé. 'Congratulations!' he cried.

2 After *dont*:

Un collègue dont je connais la sœur.

     A colleague whose sister I know.

3 Occasionally after *que*:

Le chapeau que portait la reine-mère.

     The hat the Queen Mother was wearing.

G Articles le, la, l', les

1 Sometimes the English translation omits the French *the*:

j'aime les frites	I like chips
l'amour n'est qu'un songe	love is only a dream

2 Sometimes *the* is included in the English translation and not the French translation:

Il trouvait impossible de lire à cause du bruit.
  He found it impossible to read because of the noise.

3 When dealing with parts of the body, we need to add *his/her* to the English translation.

elle se peignait *les* cheveux	she was combing *her* hair
à *la* main droite il tenait un revolver	in *his* right hand he was holding a gun

4 When descriptions such as the following are to be translated, the English requires *with*.

l'homme *au* revolver d'or	the man *with* the golden gun
la vieille dame *aux* cheveux gris	the old lady *with* grey hair
l'élève *au* visage blême	the pupil *with* the pale face

H Word for word translations

Always read the whole sentence and translate idiomatically where necessary: don't translate word for word. Some typical mistakes caused by not heeding this advice are:

l'ami des enfants	the children's friend (*not* 'the friend of the children')
il avait peur	he was frightened (*not* 'he had fear')
il faut dire la vérité	You must tell the truth (*not* 'it is necessary to tell the truth')
ils se ressemblent comme deux gouttes d'eau	they are as alike as two peas in a pod (*not* 'they are as alike as two drops of water')

I Vocabulary

Steady revision of vocabulary from this book and other sources will give you confidence to tackle the translation paper well. Collect new words and expressions and note them in a special book of your own. Have a special section for 'small' words (e.g. however, none the less, occasionally) as these are often the words it is impossible to guess from context.

Examination practice
The following test sentences are all for translation into English.

A Tenses 1 Il aimerait travailler en Turquie. **2** Je ne travaille pas en ce moment. **3** Je viens de les voir. **4** Il allait à l'école quand l'accident est arrivé. **5** Après être entré dans la salle, il m'a salué. **6** J'attendais depuis dix minutes. **7** Elle s'était levée. **8** Vous buvez un litre de vin par jour? **9** Il vint à sept heures. **10** Voilà six ans que je suis élève de ce collège. **11** Quand j'étais plus jeune, j'allais au cinéma le samedi matin, mais cela ne m'intéresse plus. **12** Je fume depuis deux ans. **13** Il fut étonné. **14** Vous veniez d'arriver, n'est-ce pas? **15** Que fera ton père quand il prendra sa retraite?

B Verb ending -ant 1 Il est descendu en se dépêchant. **2** Il est entré en courant. **3** Il est parti en se dépêchant. **4** Il est sorti en courant.

C Reflexives 1 Ce travail se fait facilement. **2** La porte s'est fermée. **3** Je me suis rasé à huit heures. **4** 'Où est-il?' s'est demandé l'agent. **5** Je me suis lavé le visage.

D On 1 On va payer? **2** On a commencé le travail à six heures. **3** On m'a dit que ... **4** On leur a demandé si ... **5** On a gagné la bataille.

E Infinitives 1 Il a décidé de partir. **2** Nous avons fini par lui dire au revoir. **3** Vous avez réussi à nous convaincre. **4** J'entends quelqu'un siffler dans cette salle de classe. **5** Regarder la télé tous les soirs? Cela ne m'intéresserait pas du tout.

F Word order 1 Un ami dont je connais la belle-sœur **2** Un auteur dont je lis très souvent les romans **3** L'impression que faisaient mes élèves étaient lamentable.

G Articles 1 Je déteste le fromage.   **2** Je trouve difficile de vous croire.   **3** La vertu a ses récompenses.   **4** L'homme à la barbe blanche.   **5** Je me suis coupé le doigt.

H Word for word translations 1 J'avais soif parce qu'il faisait chaud.   **2** Une hirondelle ne fait pas l'été.   **3** Je me sens en pleine forme – je me porte comme le Pont-Neuf!   **4** Elle est de très mauvaise humeur – elle a dû se lever du pied gauche ce matin!

I Vocabulary 1 cependant   **2** néanmoins   **3** à plusieurs reprises   **4** plutôt   **5** parfois   **6** de temps en temps   **7** toutefois   **8** autrefois   **9** plusieurs   **10** plus tard   **11** à l'heure   **12** en fin de compte   **13** auparavant   **14** selon   **15** malgré   **16** bientôt   **17** trop   **18** assez   **19** une fois   **20** actuellement.

Sample passage Below you'll find some extracts from an O level text with an imaginary candidate's attempt at a translation. Cover over the comments on p114 and work on your own version of the translation whilst at the same time looking for ways of improving on the candidate's version. When you have done all this, uncover p114 and read the comments.

A rude awakening (ox)

– Rosette, dit Mme Lebon à sa fille, tu rêves. Je ne sais pas ce que tu as depuis que tu es revenue de vacances, tu es si peu attentive.
   La jeune fille soupira. Pourquoi les vacances se terminaient-elles?

– Rosette, says Mrs Lebon to her daughter, you dream. I don't know what is the matter with you since you came back from holidays, you are a little inattentive.
   The young girl sighed. Why did holidays end (5) themselves?

Elle n'avait pas passé des vacances reposantes. Chez sa tante aussi il lui avait fallu travailler – laver la vaisselle et faire les courses. Mais par comparaison avec la vie d'ici, c'était une existence idéale.

She hadn't had restful holidays. At her aunt's too it was necessary for her to work – to do the washing-up and the errands. But by comparison with the life here, it was an existing ideal. (10)

– Et maintenant, continua sa mère, écosse-moi vite ces petits pois, sinon ils ne seront jamais cuits pour le dîner. Et laisse la casserole découverte afin qu'ils restent bien verts ... Tu m'écoutes? Rosette sursauta.

And now, continued her mother, scotch me quickly these peas, otherwise they will never be cooked for dinner. And leave the casserole uncovered, in the end they (15) are staying very green ... Are you listening to me? Rosette jumped.

– Oui, maman, dit-elle d'une voix résignée.
– Alors, dépêche-toi.

Rosette regagna la cuisine à pas lents et se contempla dans le morceau de miroir cassé qui était fixé au mur. Elle avait encore la peau bronzée, ce qui rendait ses yeux plus clairs.

- Yes, mum, she says with a resigned voice.
- Then hurry up.
    Rosette regained the kitchen in slow (20)
steps and contemplated herself in the
piece of broken minor which was
fixed to the wall. She still had
sunburnt skin which made her eyes (25)
light.

Quand elle les soulignait d'un trait noir, ils devenaient beaucoup plus expressifs. Mais pourquoi faire l'effort ici où personne ne s'intéressait à elle?

When she underlined them with a black line,
they became much more expressive. But
why make the effort here when nobody
interested himself in her?

Commentary (the line numbers refer to the student's script).

1 *dit* can mean *says*, but from the context it must be *said* (past historic); *you are dreaming* is far better than *you dream*.

2 with *depuis* it would be much better to have *what has been the matter* rather than *what is the matter*; *from holidays* sounds odd – *your holidays* sounds more natural.

4 *si* (= so) has been omitted; peu attentif, peu intéressant, peu cher would all be quite strong negatives, i.e. *in*attentive, *un*interesting, *in*expensive. Translate here as *you are so inattentive*.

5 *la jeune fille* = *girl* (not young girl); wrong tense on verb and unnecessary reflexive. Say *why were the holidays coming to an end*?

7 in English we would say *a restful holiday* and not *restful holidays*.

8 wrong tense and poor translation of *il lui avait fallu*, say *she had had to . . .*

10 slightly odd translation of *par comparaison avec*, *compared to* or *in comparison with* a little better perhaps.

11 bad mistake – the student hasn't looked at the endings of the two words *existence* and *idéale* and has forgotten that most adjectives come after their noun. Should be an *ideal existence*.

12 rather a silly guess for *écosse* but better than leaving a blank. Think about context when making a guess as well as looking for similarities with other words you know. *Écosse* has nothing to do with Scotland, but peas are *shelled*. *Quickly* would probably go in a different place in the English sentence. Where?

14 *in time for dinner* might be better; *casserole* = *pan*; *uncovered* or *with the lid off* is quite acceptable.

15 *afin que* = so that (good example of a 'small word' to note and learn of the type that often can't be guessed from context); *nice and green* is perhaps the most natural English.

17 *gave a start* is perhaps better than *jumped*.

18 *she says* should read *she said*; *in a resigned voice* or *resignedly* perhaps a little better than *with a resigned voice*.

20 *Went back to* is much better than *regained*; *slowly* would probably be quite acceptable; *gazed at* is better than *contemplated*.

24 *her skin was still tanned* would read quite well; *plus* has been omitted in translating *rendait ses yeux plus clairs* – this should read made her eyes lighter.

26 *accentuated* is perhaps the best word for *souligner*.

28 don't translate the reflexive *s'*; say *nobody was interested in her*.

Prose composition

General advice

Translation from English to French is difficult, but there are steps you can take to improve your performance.

1 The exercise is a good deal more than a word test, but the more vocabulary you know, the more confidence you will have. Revise regularly from this book and other sources; collect new vocabulary, especially 'small' words (like *cependant, mais, aussitôt*) which you come across and are easily forgotten and jot them down in a special notebook.

2 Grammatical structures and verb forms are the really difficult points in prose composition. Your performance in this part of the examination will depend directly on your revision of the grammar reference and verb tables in this book, as well as all the work you do in the same area from other sources. Make your revision regular and active. If you've forgotten what was meant by *active* turn back to the general introduction.

3 As always, you need to practise this test in timed conditions, pacing yourself to allow time for a rough version and very careful checking of the polished version.

4 You should always check for the following

  * unnecessary omissions or additions to each line of the text
  * correct choice of tense
  * correct choice of verb ending for the tense and subject – and keep a special check on perfect tense errors
  * correct positioning of adjectives (normally after noun) and agreement of adjectives with their nouns or pronouns
  * correct use of articles and their nouns (watch for silly mistakes like *la école, à le marché, des femme* which should read *à l'école, au marché, des femmes*)

Do not read through your translation checking all these five things at once. Go through five separate times, looking for one thing at a time.

Frequent points of difficulty

Many of these points are explained in the grammar reference, with test sentences for practice. Concentrate on those test sentences which ask you to translate from English into French to prepare yourself for the prose composition test in the examination. On pp118–9 there are some passages which have been set by Examination Boards. When attempting these try and spot the points they are testing. Knowing what the trap is is the best way of avoiding it!

1 Changed word order after direct speech (p108)
2 Various tenses of *pouvoir*, *devoir*, *savoir*, *vouloir* (p108) (see verb tables)
3 There are at least two different verbs for *know* in French
  (a) *connaître* to know, be familiar with a person/place
      je connais Paris; il connaît mon père
  (b) *savoir* to know a fact, have knowledge of
      il ne savait pas que son père était déjà parti
        he did not know that his father had already left
4 There are two verbs to express *can* in French
  (a) *pouvoir* to be allowed to, have permission to
      je peux sortir tout seul   I can go out on my own
  (b) *savoir* to know how to, be able (physically)
      je sais parler français; je sais nager
5 *Penser à, penser de*   Remember the difference in meaning between these two verbs
  je pense à ma mère
    I am thinking about (my thoughts are turning towards) my mother
  Qu'est-ce que tu penses de mon chapeau?
    What do you think of (what is your opinion of) my new hat?
6 The imperative or command form of the verb (see verb tables)
7 Prepositions following verbs (p39)
8 Negatives (pp30–32)
9 *Avoir* and *faire* expressions (pp26–7)
10 Infinitive constructions (p108)
11 *Venir de* + *infinitive* (p106)
12 *Depuis* constructions with *present* and *imperfect* (p106)
13 *Pendant* with past time; *pour* with future time (p38)
14 Intelligent enough to . . . strong enough to . . . (p38)

15   *With + parts of the body*
     the girl *with* fair hair   la jeune fille *aux* cheveux blonds
     the boy *with* the injured arm   le garçon *au* bras blessé
     the man *with* a white beard   l'homme *à* la barbe blanche
16   500 km *from* Paris . . . (p37)
17   It was + to + *infinitive*; *il* + *être* + *de* + *infinitive*
     It was difficult *to find* an immediate solution.
     Il était difficile *de trouver* une solution immédiate.
     It was impossible *to carry* on with the journey.
     Il était impossible *de continuer* le voyage.
18   *à cause de + noun; parce que + verb*
     A cause du mauvais temps, on a annulé le match.
       Because of the bad weather, the match was cancelled.
     On a annulé le match parce qu'il faisait mauvais.
       The match was cancelled because the weather was bad.
     A cause de sa faute, tout le monde a souffert.
       Because of his mistake, everyone suffered.
     Tout le monde a souffert parce qu'il avait fait une faute.
       Everyone suffered because he had made a mistake.
19   *pendant + noun; pendant que + verb*
     Pendant notre visite Jacques est tombé malade.
       During our visit Jacques fell ill.
     Pendant que nous visitions Paris, Jacques est tombé malade.
       Whilst we were visiting Paris, Jacques fell ill.
20   Omission of *un/une* with professions
     ma sœur est infirmière   my sister is a nurse
     je suis institutrice   I'm a primary school teacher
     il voulait devenir médecin   he wanted to become a doctor
21   Need for *que* after *verbs of thinking*, *telling* and *noticing*
     Il *a dit que* j'avais raison.
       He said I was right.
     J'*ai expliqué que* j'avais oublié mon parapluie.
       I explained I had forgotten my umbrella.
22   *Verb of motion + up/down/across/in/out*
     (a) use *en* + the present participle of the verb (to form the present
         participle take the *nous* form of present tense and substitute
         -ant for *-ons* = demand*ons*, demand*ant*)
     (b) to translate *ran across, rushed out, ran in, ran out*, etc, translate
         the *across, in, out* as a verb and turn the *ran, rushed*, etc, into a
         present participle

   (c) hence
       he *ran across* the road   il *a traversé* la rue *en courant*
       he *hurried into* the room   il *est entré* dans la pièce *en se
                                          dépêchant*

Examination practice
The following passages are all for translation into French.

1 That night John went to bed late. When he opened his eyes he saw
  that it was already half past eight. He had to be at the factory at nine
  o'clock. He got up, dressed himself and decided not to shave. He
  drank a cup of coffee and dashed into the street.
    There was nobody there. Even the newspaper-seller who was
  usually on the corner had already left. John started to wait for the bus.
  A quarter of an hour later he was still there, and he had only seen a
  few children. Finally he saw a taxi which stopped almost immediately.
    John got in and the taxi started off. 'Go as fast as you can,' said
  John to the driver. 'Fortunately there isn't much traffic.' The man
  seemed surprised. When they got to the factory, John saw that the
  doors were closed. Then he remembered that it was Sunday. He went
  back home on foot.   (OX)

2 About four years ago, I was walking along the pavement when
  suddenly I noticed an old friend sitting in front of a café on the other
  side of the street.
    As I had not seen him recently, I crossed the street to speak to
  him. 'Hullo, how are you?' I asked him. 'What are you doing here?
  Are you waiting for someone?'
    'No, nobody,' he replied, shaking my hand. 'I arrived in town last
  night. I've just finished my studies and I'm taking a few days'
  holiday before looking for a job.'
    After chatting for a long time we decided to have lunch together
  in a nearby restaurant we knew quite well. During the meal, he
  invited me to go and see him that evening.   (WEL)

3 It was dark when they entered the castle. They went up two floors and
  came to a long corridor where there were many rooms. 'On the
  right,' whispered Victor – 'the fourth room at the end.' They soon
  found the door but it was locked. After about ten minutes they were
  able to open it, and went in. Beauchamp saw the bed where his father
  was sleeping. He woke him up gently. 'It's me, Philippe, and a
  friend. Don't be afraid. Get up, but don't say a word.' The father

got dressed, but as they were about to leave the room, he said in a low voice: 'I'm not the only prisoner here. There is also a girl, but I don't know her.' 'It's probably Mademoiselle Boudard,' said Victor. 'I don't know her, but I have seen her several times in the park.' 'Do you know where her room is?' 'Yes, I think it's opposite mine.' 'That's the blue room,' murmured Victor. 'It will not be too difficult to open that door.'

Beauchamp's father went into the room and five minutes later he came out with the girl and said to Victor and his son: 'You are right; it is Mademoiselle Boudard.' They all went quietly downstairs and came out on to the terrace where their friends were waiting. (SUJB)

4 Susan Thorpe was waiting for Colette, her French pen-friend, at London Airport. It was twenty past ten and Colette's aeroplane had just arrived, a little late. Soon Susan saw a girl with fair hair who looked very elegant. She smiled. 'It's Susan, isn't it?' Susan, who was wearing trousers and an old shirt, blushed and replied: 'Yes, I am Susan. I hope you will be happy with us. Come with me; daddy is over there in the car.'

During the journey Colette asked her friend a lot of questions. She wanted to know if Susan went to the theatre, if she went out much in the evening, if she smoked, and if history interested her. Poor Susan, who was very fond of sport and who did not like reading, decided that the visit was not a very good idea after all. However, she was wrong; the two girls spent a very pleasant month together and then they went to France. (OX)

Comprehension (including Use of French)

Most of the examinations set by the different Boards include some type of comprehension test, whether reading or listening, with questions and answers either in French or English, multiple-choice or other types. This section gives you advice on tackling some of the important types of comprehension tests, with some material for you to practise at home.

Reading comprehension
A With questions and answers in French
1 This type of test not only requires you to understand a passage of French but to show that you can use French correctly in your answers. Some Exam Boards call this type of test 'Use of French'.

2 Because you are being tested on two things at once, it is very easy to make mistakes in your French. Pace yourself to allow for a rough version, with time in hand at the end to go through your final version several times making separate checks for the following: correct tense usage; correct ending on all parts of the verb for the tense and subject, especially past participles of *être* verbs; correct position and agreement of adjectives; correct use of articles (*le/la/l'/les*, etc) for singular and plural. Do not mis-spell any words given in the text or questions. Examiners are inclined to react severely if you do.

3 Read carefully any instructions about what tenses to use or about answering in complete sentences.

4 Base your answers on the information in the passage. You shouldn't have to invent material which isn't there, unless you are asked to express a general opinion.

5 Don't waste time by giving overlong, irrelevant answers, which will gain you no extra marks. *If* you are confident in the use of pronouns (pp40–42) use them to shorten your answers.

6 On the whole, the questions are designed so that you cannot just copy answers from the text. Study carefully the following examples of ways in which your usage of French can be tested by forcing you to alter what is printed in the text.

1 Having to make a change of tense

(a)

Text Les Lenoir ont été très déçus de leurs vacances au camping de St Gingolphe. *Il pleuvait* déjà depuis deux jours quand ils se sont mis en route, et il a continué à pleuvoir pendant deux semaines de suite.

Qn Quel temps avait-il fait le jour de leur départ?

Rep *Il avait plu* ce jour-là.

(b)

Text La voiture est entrée en collision avec un autobus, *après avoir dérapé* à cause du verglas.

Qn Qu'est-ce qui était arrivé à la voiture avant d'entrer en collision avec l'autobus?

Rep *Elle avait dérapé* à cause du verglas.

(c)

Text *Il n'avait pas encore fini* son dîner quand on a sonné à la porte.

Qn Qu'est-ce qu'il faisait quand on a sonné à la porte?

Rep *Il finissait* son dîner.

(d)

Text Son rêve de *devenir* médecin dépendait des résultats de son examen.

Qn Qu'est-ce qui arriverait s'il réussissait à ses examens?

Rep Il *deviendrait* médecin.

(e)

Text En quittant sa mère il lui a dit qu'il *rentrerait* à sept heures.

Qn Quels étaient ses mots exacts en quittant sa mère?

Rep 'Je *rentrerai* à sept heures.'

2 Having to change the subject of the sentence

Text '*Nous* passer*ons* deux semaines en Tunisie,' ont dit les Chalon.

Qn Que feront les Chalon?

Rep *Ils* passer*ont* deux semaines en Tunisie.

3 Having to change the subject and related parts in the sentence

Text '*Je* vais *me* baigner, puis lire *mon* magazine,' a-t-elle dit à sa mère.

Qn Qu'est-ce qu'elle allait faire?

Rep *Elle* allait *se* baigner, puis lire *son* magazine.

4 Questions with venir de + infinitive (see p106)

(a)

Text Philippe est rentré en France après des vacances en Allemagne.

Qn Qu'est-ce que Philippe vient de faire en Allemagne?

Rep Il vient d'y passer ses vacances.

(b)

Text Michel avait acheté récemment une nouvelle voiture.

Qn Qu'est-ce que Michel venait de faire?

Rep Il venait d'acheter une nouvelle auto.

5 Questions with depuis (see p43)

(a)

Text 'Je serai triste de quitter mon poste à la banque après trois années très heureuses,' a dit Mlle Corbeau.

Qn Depuis combien de temps Mlle Corbeau travaille-t-elle à la banque?

Rep Elle y travaille depuis trois ans.

(b)

Text 'Je m'excuse, monsieur. Je sais qu'il est déjà midi et quart et que vous êtes arrivé à onze heures. C'est que j'ai dû m'occuper de beaucoup de gens ce matin.'

Qn Ce client attend depuis une heure et quart maintenant. Et à onze heures et demie?

Rep Il attend*ait* depuis une demi-heure. (He *had been* waiting)

6 Questions which force you to give a negative answer (see pp30–32)

(a)

Text Robert était enfant unique, ce qui expliquait peut-être son isolement.

Qn Combien de frères avait Robert?

Rep Il n'avait pas de frères. (*or* Il n'en avait pas.)

(b)

Text Le salon était vide.

Qn Qui était dans le salon.

Rep Personne n'était dans le salon. (*or* Il n'y avait personne dans le salon.)

(c)

Text Le groupe était parti sans accompagnateurs.

Qn Qui accompagnait le groupe?

Rep Personne ne l'accompagnait. (*or* Il n'y avait pas d'accompagnateurs.)

(d)

Text Nicole a cherché partout dans la maison, mais en vain.

Qn Qu'est-ce que Nicole a trouvé?

Rep Elle n'a rien trouvé.

Some final points

1 You will be able to give relevant, correct answers only if you are sure about interrogatives (see pp32–3). Take care especially not to mix up questions with some form of *qui* (who?) and *que* (what?).

2 Look out for clues like 'pour quelle*s* raison*s* . . .?' showing that more than one piece of information is required for full marks.

3 If the marks allocated to each question are printed on the paper this can provide a guide to you as to how much detail is needed in each answer.

Two test passages (AEB, June 1978)

(**a**) – Vous avez trouvé l'argent?

– Oui.

– Alors, rendez-moi mon fils!

– Pas encore, j'ai toujours quelques problèmes. Je vous rapellerai.

– Ah non!

Mais trop tard. Il avait raccroché.

Christophe avait été enlevé trois jours auparavant, en se rendant à l'école. Un inconnu l'avait poussé dans une camionnette. Christophe ne voulait plus que l'on accompagne parce que, comme il disait, il était 'devenu grand' – il allait avoir neuf ans à la fin du mois. Presque immédiatement après l'enlèvement, une voix jeune, excitée, avait téléphoné à ma femme et réclamé un million de francs de rançon. 'Vous n'informerez ni la police ni la presse si vous voulez revoir votre garçon en vie.' Moi, j'étais à Paris, et mon père à Rome, quand ma femme nous a prévenus, mais nous sommes rentrés immédiatement tous les deux: nous savions qu'il ne plaisantait pas.

1 Qu'est-ce que le narrateur avait espéré en donnant de l'argent au 'kidnapper'?

2 Pourquoi le 'kidnapper' ne rendait-il pas le petit garçon?

3 Comment savez-vous que ce coup de téléphone ne devait pas être le dernier?

4 Que faisait Christophe quand on l'a enlevé?

5 Quel âge avait-il au moment de l'enlèvement?

6 Qu'est-ce que le 'kidnapper' menaçait de faire?

7 Comment le narrateur a-t-il appris la nouvelle de l'enlèvement?

(**b**) Georges alluma une cigarette, puis regarda par la fenêtre de son bureau. Il venait de reprendre sa place quand la porte s'ouvrit brusquement. C'était Henriette, sa femme.

– Que fais-tu là? demanda-t-il d'un ton sévère.

Sans rien dire, elle s'assit dans un fauteuil, et regarda son mari, qui ne cessait pas de lire ses documents. Puis elle sursauta.

– Oh, que je suis bête! J'ai laissé la porte de la maison ouverte!

– C'est pour ça que tu es venue me déranger? Tu ne comprends pas que j'ai du travail à faire? Je m'occupe d'un cas très intéressant – c'est un homme qui a probablement empoisonné sa femme.

– Charmant!

– Oui, mais veux-tu attendre un instant?

Elle dut attendre dix minutes, et en attendant, elle parcourut des yeux la vieille bibliothèque remplie de livres très anciens. Enfin Georges se leva.

– Alors, qu'est-ce que c'est?

– Je suis venue simplement pour . . .

– Oui, je sais. Tu es venue essayer de me persuader . . .

– De me donner un peu d'argent, c'est tout.

– C'est vraiment tout?

– Mais ou.

– Alors voici mille francs. Maintenant laisse-moi tranquille. Je travaille. A tout à l'heure.

    Et Henriette sortit, très contente.

(NB do *not* use the past historic tense, e.g. *il donna*, in your answers.)

   8 A quel moment Georges a-t-il regardé par la fenêtre?
   9 Qu'est-ce qu'Henriette a fait tout de suite après être entrée dans le bureau?
  10 Qu'est-ce qu'elle n'avait pas fait en quittant la maison?
  11 Quel travail Georges était-il en train de faire?
  12 Comment Henriette a-t-elle passé les dix minutes pendant lesquelles elle a dû attendre.
  13 Qu'est-ce qu'elle est venue faire au bureau?
  14 Après lui avoir donné l'argent, qu'est-ce que Georges a dit à Henriette de faire?

B Reading comprehension with questions/answers in English

1 Many of the points made above apply equally to this type of test, in particular the special instructions given about how to form your answers.

2 Be careful not to make your answers overlong. Because you may be able to say more in English there is a temptation to include irrelevant material, and you will be penalized for this.

C Reading comprehension with multiple-choice answers

1 No writing in French or English is required in this test. You are asked to choose an answer usually from four or five possible options, and these – depending on the Board – can be in either French or English. There is normally a special grid for you to fill in your choice. If possible have a good look at one of these answer grids before your examination (your school should have some) so that you are familiar with the layout.

2 Do not think that you have plenty of time because you are not doing any writing. You need the time to *read*, *think* and *mark in* your answers carefully against the correct question number.

3 Never leave a blank and never mark in two answers.

4 Pace yourself to allow time for tackling the longer passages which follow the short items that frequently start the test.

5 Do not panic if there are some difficult words which you don't understand at first. You may be able to work them out from the context or you may even be able to get the right answer without understanding that particular word. Panic can lead you to make other mistakes, so keep calm!

6 Study with equal care the *text*, the *questions* and *all* the possible answers. You will score badly if you miss out on any of these.

7 You are asked to choose the most likely answer, not the one which someone with a Monty Python sense of humour would choose. On the other hand, beware an answer which looks *immediately* obviously correct.

Three major sources of error

1 Misreading the person in the question, e.g. reading *elle lui dit* as *he says to her* instead of *she says to him*.

2 Misreading a tense, e.g. answering *qu'est-ce qu'il ferait* with a sentence about what someone *did*, rather than what someone *would do*.

3 Falling for an incorrect connection between a word in the text and a word in an answer. Often the two words may look alike. A silly example – in the text: Robert voulait du *pain* (he wanted some bread), in an answer: Robert était malade (he was ill – in *pain*).

Choose your answer, but also try and work out why you might have wrongly selected the other possible answers. See if your answers and conclusions match the ones on pp128–31.

Short items

Select the answer which is most likely to the question or remark in the given situation:

1 Une jeune fille avait fait un échange scolaire en Angleterre. A son retour, sa camarade de classe lui a demandé:
  (a) J'espère que tu t'amuseras bien?

  (b) Est-ce qu'on échange souvent des écoles en Angleterre?
  (c) La famille était-elle gentille?
  (d) Je me suis bien amusée en Angleterre, n'est-ce pas?

2 Une jeune femme a été témoin d'un accident de la route. Un agent lui dit:
  (a) Il faut que vous alliez à l'hôpital pour y être soignée.
  (b) Voulez-vous me décrire ce qui s'est passé?
  (c) Vous devriez conduire avec plus de précaution.
  (d) Vous avez subi beaucoup d'accidents?

3 Un étranger arrêta un passant dans la rue et lui demanda: 'Pardon monsieur, voulez-vous m'indiquer le chemin de l'hôtel de ville s'il vous plaît?' L'autre lui répondit:
  (a) Oui monsieur. Combien de nuits voulez-vous y passer?
  (b) Volontiers monsieur. Troisième à gauche et première à droite.
  (c) Avec plaisir. Le chemin de fer est tout près.
  (d) De rien, monsieur. Je suis à votre service.

4 Maman entre dans la chambre de son fils à moitié endormi et lui dit de se lever. Le garçon répond:
  (a) Ah, que tu es fatiguée.
  (b) Je suis toujours endormi.
  (c) Je cherche l'autre moitié.
  (d) J'ai encore sommeil.

Longer passages

Read the following passages carefully. A number of questions, followed by four suggested answers, are given after each passage. Select the most appropriate answer by referring closely to the passage. Read the whole passage before attempting the answers.

A Mme X est furieuse. Elle vient d'échouer à la moitié de son permis de conduire.
– Il y a tant d'accidents! On a recommandé aux examinateurs d'être sévères. Ils font tout pour nous refuser.
  Avec les autres candidats, Mme X a attendu plus d'une heure sous la pluie. Elle frissonnait donc quand son tour est venu. Les six candidats qui la précédaient, tous des jeunes, ont été recalés: les garçons pour le

code, les filles pour la conduite. Elle monte dans la voiture et doit at tendre deux minutes. Puis l'examinateur a commencé l'épreuve:
– Voyons le code! Où y a-t-il des feux clignotants rouges?

1 Pourquoi Mme X est-elle furieuse?
  (a) Elle a échoué complètement à son examen de permis de conduire.
  (b) Elle n'a réussi qu'à une partie de l'examen.
  (c) Elle a eu un accident.
  (d) Elle n'a pas passé l'examen.

2 Pourquoi les examinateurs ne laissent-ils pas réussir tous les candidats?
  (a) Parce qu'ils aiment être sévères.
  (b) Parce qu'on ne leur a pas permis de conduire.
  (c) Parce qu'ils prennent plaisir à refuser des candidats.
  (d) Parce qu'ils veulent réduire le nombre d'accidents.

3 Pourquoi Mme X frissonnait-elle?
  (a) Parce qu'elle était trempée.
  (b) Parce qu'elle attendait depuis presque une heure.
  (c) Parce qu'elle avait fait un tour.
  (d) Parce qu'il faisait froid.

4 Pour quelle raison les jeunes filles n'ont-elles pas réussi à l'examen?
  (a) Elles ne s'étaient pas conduites comme il faut.
  (b) Elles ne savaient pas le code de la route.
  (c) Elles ne savaient pas très bien conduire.
  (d) Elles étaient trop jeunes pour conduire.

B Zut! il pleut! Cette exclamation résumait, hier matin, l'état d'esprit des Parisiens, et des banlieusards surtout. Pour ceux qui habitent 'hors les murs' une grève des autobus n'est à peu près acceptable que lorsqu'elle leur fournit une belle promenade par un temps printanier.

De fait, si la température s'était adoucie, le ciel gris n'incitait pas à l'optimisme le million de voyageurs qui attendaient en vain, aux portes de Paris et ailleurs, les autobus. Si, aux premières heures de la matinée, il y eut des queues aux têtes de ligne, elles furent très réduites et souvent inexistantes dans Paris, les usagers ayant été prévenus de la grève des autobus par la presse du matin.

1 Pourquoi a-t-on juré en voyant le temps qu'il faisait?
  (a) On devrait prendre l'autobus au lieu de faire une belle promenade.
  (b) Ce serait une perte de temps.
  (c) Le temps était printanier.
  (d) On allait se faire mouiller en allant à pied.

2 Pourquoi cette grève était-elle sérieuse surtout pour les banlieusards?
  (a) Ils ne voulaient pas l'accepter.
  (b) Les fournisseurs étaient déjà en grève.
  (c) L'autobus était en mauvais état.
  (d) Ils avaient une longue distance à parcourir.

3 Quel temps faisait-il ce matin-là?
  (a) Il faisait froid.
  (b) Il faisait moins froid que le jour précédent.
  (c) Il y avait quelques petits nuages gris au ciel.
  (d) Il faisait un beau temps printanier.

4 Où attendaient les voyageurs?
  (a) Ils attendaient à la porte de leur maison.
  (b) Ils attendaient ailleurs.
  (c) Ils attendaient à la périphérie de la ville.
  (d) Ils attendaient en vain.

Key to answers and comments

Short items **1** (a) incorrect; 'I hope you will enjoy yourself' is clearly the wrong tense if the girl has already done the exchange. (b) incorrect; 'Do they often exchange schools in England?' does not make sense, but the unwary candidate might make a wrong connection between *échange*, which here is a verb, and *échange scolaire* (school exchange) which is mentioned in the question stem. (c) correct 'Was the family nice?' (d) incorrect; 'I enjoyed myself in England' is the remark which the girl herself might make, not her friend who is asking her about the exchange. **2** (a) incorrect; a witness (*témoin*) to an accident would not have to go to hospital. (b) correct; the policeman asked for a description of what happened. (c) incorrect; a policeman would not caution a witness about his or her driving. (d) incorrect; a witness would not be asked if he or she had had other accidents, but some candidates might be distracted by the word *accidents* which occurs in this answer and in the question stem. **3** (a) incorrect; 'How many nights do you wish to stay?' is meant to distract those who think *hôtel de ville* is some sort of hotel rather than the town hall. (b) correct; directions to the town hall are given. (c) incorrect; the railway is now mentioned, with the possibility of a wrong connection between *le chemin de* ... (the way to ...) in the question stem and *le chemin de fer* (railway) in this answer. (d) incorrect; 'Don't mention it' would make sense after the directions had been given and the stranger had expressed his gratitude. It does not make sense at this point in the conversation. **4** (a) incorrect; 'How tired you are' does not make sense as the boy's reply, although she might have said it to him (without the feminine agreement!) (b) incorrect; 'I am still asleep' is a physical impossibility, but note the connection in printed form, between *à moitié endormi* (half asleep) in the question stem and *endormi* (asleep) in this answer. (c) 'I am looking for the other half' is somewhat cryptic, but again the word *moitié* is there to distract you. (d) correct; 'I'm still tired' does make sense. Longer passages **A1** (a) incorrect; we are told she has only half failed, so the word *complètement* rules out this possibility, although the rest of the wording is similar in the passage and in this answer. (b) correct; she has only passed one part of her exam. (c) incorrect; there is no suggestion at all that she has had an accident, although the high number of accidents is mentioned in the passage. (d) incorrect; *passer un examen* is to take an exam, not to pass it, an old trap. (**2**) (a) incorrect; Mme X claims they are strict, but there is no evidence from the passage that they enjoy being strict. (b) incorrect; 'Because they weren't allowed to drive' makes no sense at all, although a confused candidate might make a wrong connection with the noun *permis de conduire* (driving licence) in the passage. (c) incorrect; again there is no evidence that they enjoy failing candidates in the statement '*Ils font tout pour nous refuser.*' (d) correct; the advice to examiners to be strict is juxtaposed in the passage with the reference to the number of accidents as an explanation of their severity. **3** (a) correct; she had been waiting in the rain and therefore (*donc*) was shivering. (b) incorrect; the word hour is mentioned in the passage, but she had been waiting for more than an hour (*plus d'une heure*) not nearly an hour (*presque une heure*). (c) incorrect; there is no mention in the passage that she had been for a walk (*faire un tour*) although there is a reference to her turn coming (*son tour est venu*). (d) incorrect; shivering could be wrongly connected with cold, but no mention of cold is made in the passage. **4** (a) incorrect; there is no suggestion that they had behaved badly (*elles ne s'étaient pas conduites comme il faut*) in the passage, but note the similarity in printed form, not meaning, between *se conduire* (to behave) and *conduire* (to drive). (b) incorrect; the highway code is mentioned, but it was the young men who were failed on this part of the exam, not the girls. (c) correct; they couldn't drive very well as they were failed for their driving (*conduite*). (d) incorrect; there is no suggestion that they were failed because of being too young, although the passage does say that the candidates who were failed were all young.

B1 (a) incorrect; 'They would have to catch a bus' cannot make sense when the passage is all about a bus strike. The words in the passage *faire une belle promenade* might still draw some candidates to this answer. (b) incorrect; there is no reference in the passage to any waste of time (*perte de temps*) although the word *temps* (meaning weather here) is used in the question stem. (c) incorrect; there is no statement in the passage about the weather being spring like, only that strikes are more acceptable to the Parisians in that type of weather. (d) correct; the commuters were going to get soaked going to work on foot. **2** (a) incorrect; 'They refused to accept it' does not make sense as a reply to 'Why was it serious?' although the word *acceptable* does occur in the passage to distract the student (the strikes are just about acceptable in spring weather). (b) incorrect; there is no reference to any suppliers (*fournisseurs*) being on strike, although there is a word in the passage meant to distract – *fournit* (... when it supplies them with ...). (c) incorrect; 'The bus was in a bad state' (*en mauvais état*) does not make sense. The word *état* is used to talk about the state of mind (*état d'esprit*) of the Parisians in the opening lines of the passage. (d) correct; people living in the suburbs (*banlieusards*) do have a long distance to travel to work. **3** (a) incorrect; a reference is made to temperature, but not to the coldness of the weather. (b) correct; the temperature had become milder (*s'était adoucie*). (c) incorrect; the words grey and sky are mentioned in the passage, but not with reference to small grey clouds in the sky, rather to describe a grey, overcast sky. (d) incorrect; the weather was not spring like, although the words *temps printanier* occur in the passage as already mentioned to describe the weather conditions most suited to a bus strike. **4** (a) incorrect; there is no statement to the effect that the passengers were waiting outside their own front doors, only to their waiting *aux portes de Paris*, the 'gates' of the city of Paris. (b) incorrect; 'elsewhere' is a rather unhelpful answer to the question. (c) correct; we have been told that these passengers live 'outside the walls' (*hors les murs*) or 'gates' of the city, so they must be waiting on the outskirts (*la périphérie*). (d) incorrect; they waited in vain does not answer the question 'where?'

Listening comprehension

A Tests involving listening to a longer passage, followed by printed questions

1 Generally the passage is read to you a first time before you are allowed to see the questions. On this first time through, try and sort out the overall meaning, not worrying if there are some difficult words. You may not be asked about them.

2 Once you have read the questions carefully, you know what to listen out for in a really concentrated way in the second reading.

3 Exact procedure for the second reading varies; sometimes the text is split into several sections with a pause after each in which you write your answers. You may or may not be allowed to take notes during the reading. Usually you have a chance to hear the passage a final time after which you are given time to fill in any blanks or change any answers.

4 Whether answering in French or English follow carefully any special instructions; be concise and relevant. Check your French as on p115.

The following practice passage is to be read to you by someone else either 'live' or on tape. Do not look at the passage yourself, nor look at the questions before your practice. Listen to the passage once. Spend three minutes studying the questions. Listen to the passage a second time. Spend about twenty minutes trying to answer the questions in English. Check your answers in the answer section right at the back of the book and go over the passage in detail.

Ce jour-là vers cinq heures du matin le soleil qui entrait dans la chambre que j'occupais chez mon oncle Marcel, instituteur du village de Marsac, m'a réveillé brusquement.

Ma chambre avec son plafond blanc et ses meubles de bois blanc avait une certaine gaîté que j'aimais beaucoup. Je me suis mis à la fenêtre et j'ai regardé la rivière qui coulait au milieu des champs verts de la vallée. Le vent frais me caressait le visage, les murmures de la rivière et des arbres semblaient m'appeler. Tout à coup j'ai pensé aux poissons qui m'attendaient là-bas et une folle envie d'aller à la pêche m'a pris. Pourtant mon oncle m'avait défendu d'aller à la rivière tout seul. Mes parents étaient restés chez nous à Paris et mon oncle se sentait responsable pour moi. Tous les jours à la première page de son journal on parlait d'enfants qui s'étaient noyés dans des rivières.

J'ai ouvert ma porte doucement. Pour sortir il me fallait traverser la chambre de mon oncle. J'ai avancé sur la pointe des pieds craignant de réveiller avec le bruit de mes gros souliers mon oncle qui dormait encore. Et j'ai tremblé quand j'ai entendu sonner la cloche de l'église. Mon oncle Marcel m'aurait certainement empêché d'aller là-bas sur le bord de la rivière.

Mais il dormait d'un profond sommeil. Je regrettais de le tromper, de me sauver ainsi. Je me suis arrêté un instant à regarder son visage calme que le repos rendait plus doux. Ma première pensée a été de lui crier: 'Lève-toi, mon oncle. Allons au bord de la rivière. L'air du matin te fera du bien. Tu auras bon appétit au retour.'

Mais je ne lui ai rien dit et lentement à petits pas j'ai gagné la porte. Je suis descendu par l'escalier et je suis sorti dans le jardin. (SCE)

1 Why and at what time did the author wake up? (2)
2 What was the profession of the person he was living with? (1)
3 Describe his bedroom. (3)
4 Describe the view from the window. (3)
5 What thought suddenly came into the author's mind and what did he wish to do? (2)
6 What had his uncle forbidden him to do and why? (5)
7 Describe how he left his bedroom and went through his uncle's room. (2)
8 Why were such precautions necessary? (2)
9 What did he hear and what was his reaction to it? (2)
10 What do you know of his uncle's facial appearance at this time? (2)
11 What was the author tempted to shout to his uncle? (4)
12 After leaving his uncle's room what did he do? (2)

(Marks for each question are given in brackets)

B Tests with multiple-choice answers in French or English

1 Most of the hints given on pp124–5, for tackling multiple-choice reading comprehension, also apply here.
2 Tests on tape require you to develop nerves of steel! Try and get in plenty of practice, especially if your school will let you work on tapes in the language laboratory in your own time.
3 If you think you have got an answer wrong, forget about it and concentrate fully on the next question. Worrying will not help and may even cause you to get the next question wrong.
4 If you do have some time to spare in between questions have a look at the next set of possible answers.
5 When tackling the longer passages do not despair if you are baffled after the first reading. Once you have had a chance to hear the questions for the first time you will be able to concentrate on the particular points raised. It is probably better to wait until you have heard the questions a second time before marking in your answer, although you may be able to narrow down your choice after you have first heard the questions.
6 Listening comprehension is a very difficult test and needs lots of practice inside and outside the classroom. Never miss a chance to listen to some French, however little you understand at first. Try the language programmes put out by radio and television, French films with English subtitles or even French pop music radio stations on long wave on your transistor.

Sources of error

The traps are similar to those in multiple-choice reading tests, especially misunderstanding who is supposed to be saying what to whom and not listening to the tense. The most common mistake is wrongly connecting a word on the tape and a word on the answer paper. You saw how in the reading tests words which looked alike were intended to confuse you; in the listening tests words which sound alike are put in to distract you. Look carefully at some examples of this in the following extract from a test. (The extract is from a passage about a man who has just bought a new car and finds it difficult to concentrate on his work because of this.)

Words on tape   Au travail je n'ai pu m'empêcher de rêver continuellement de mon nouvel achat. Que la journée était ennuyeuse! Cinq heures et demie enfin!

Question on tape Que faisait M. Grimaud pendant la journée?

Possible answers   (a) Il pensait au plaisir d'aller pêcher.

                   (b) Il rêvait à son nouveau chat.

                   (c) Il passait son temps à penser à ce qu'il venait d'acheter.

                   (d) Ne pouvant pas travailler, il regardait continuellement sa nouvelle montre.

Comment on possible answers (a) incorrect; M. Grimaud was not thinking about the pleasure of going fishing (. . . *plaisir d'aller pêcher*); there is a connection in sound but not meaning between *pêcher* and *empêcher* (to prevent) which is designed to confuse candidates. (b) incorrect; he was not thinking of his new cat (*son nouveau chat*) although again there is a similarity of sound between *chat* and *achat* (purchase). (c) correct; he did spend time thinking about what he had just bought as we are told that he couldn't prevent himself from continually dreaming of his new purchase (*je n'ai pu m'empêcher de rêver continuellement de mon nouvel achat*). (d) incorrect; we are not told in the passage that he kept looking at his new watch, although candidates might be drawn towards this choice by references towards the boring nature of the day (*Que la journée était ennuyeuse!*) and the time seeming to drag until 5.30 (*Cinq heures et demie enfin!*). There is no specific reference to his looking at any new watch, however.

Practice listening passage

This passage is about half the length of an actual exam passage. You will need someone's help either to read it to you 'live' or record it on cassette when you are out of the room. Do not look at the passage yourself.

1 You will need (a) this book, closed at first and (b) a sheet of paper for making notes and writing down the letter you choose each time for your answer.
2 Your helper should read the passage straight through twice, or the tape should be played twice.
3 After the second reading, open the book and start answering the questions, taking care to keep the passage covered.
4 After ten minutes listen to the passage a third time.
5 After the third time you have about three minutes to fill in any missing answers or alter any answers.
6 Check your answers against the ones right at the back of the book. Try and work out each time why they hoped you might be misled by the incorrect answers, on the lines of the example from the previous listening test.

Robert King avait passé la moitié de la nuit à achever un travail qu'il considérait ennuyeux. Il ne s'était couché qu'à trois heures du matin et essayait de rattraper le temps perdu. Son ami Georges était sorti de bonne heure: il avait une course à faire à l'autre bout de Paris. Vers huit heures, le concierge, qui montait les lettres, frappa. D'habitude il n'insistait pas et les glissait sous la porte. Mais ce matin-là il continua de frapper. Robert, mal éveillé, alla ouvrir en grommelant; il n'entendit pas ce que le concierge lui disait à propos d'un article de journal, et prit les lettres sans les regarder. Poussant la porte sans la fermer, il se recoucha et se rendormit.

Une heure après, il fut de nouveau réveillé par des pas dans sa chambre: il eut la stupéfaction de voir, au pied de son lit, une figure inconnue qui le saluait gravement. Un journaliste, qui avait trouvé la porte ouverte, était entré sans frapper. Robert, furieux, sauta du lit:
– Qu'est-ce que vous venez faire ici?

Il avait saisi son oreiller pour le jeter sur le nouveau-venu qui fit un mouvement de retraite. Ils s'expliquèrent. Un reporter de la *Nation* voulait discuter avec Monsieur King l'article paru dans le *Matin*.

1 Robert had gone to bed late because

    (a) he considered it a bore to go to bed early.
    (b) he thought it better to do so when he was working.
    (c) half the night had passed before he realized the time.
    (d) he had had to finish off a boring piece of work.
    (e) he had been unable to complete his work.

2 He was now trying

    (a) to make up the time he had lost.
    (b) to see what the weather was like.
    (c) to find his watch, which he had lost.
    (d) to catch up on his work.
    (e) to catch an early train.

3 Why had Georges gone out early?

    (a) He was attending a course.
    (b) He had business on the other side of the city.
    (c) He didn't know his way about Paris.
    (d) He was playing golf at the other end of Paris.
    (e) He was going to the races in Paris.

4 What happened at about eight o'clock?

    (a) The post was brought up by the cleaning-woman.
    (b) The postman knocked.
    (c) The caretaker counted the letters.
    (d) Georges went out to get the post.
    (e) The caretaker knocked.

5 Generally the letters were

    (a) pushed through the box.
    (b) left outside the door.
    (c) slipped under the door.
    (d) collected at the door.
    (e) slipped under the mat.

6 As he went to the door, Robert was

    (a) badly shaken.
    (b) wide awake.
    (c) fumbling for his dressing-gown.
    (d) hardly awake.
    (e) feeling well.

7 As he took the letters, he was told something about

  (a) the newspaper which should have been delivered.
  (b) the caretaker.
  (c) a newspaper article.
  (d) an article he had ordered.
  (e) what the letters contained.

8 Before Robert went back to bed, he

  (a) shut the door with a bang.
  (b) pushed the letters through the door.
  (c) took the letters to his desk.
  (d) pushed the door shut.
  (e) omitted to shut the door.

9 What woke him up an hour later?

  (a) The sight of a stranger at the foot of his bed.
  (b) Footsteps on the landing.
  (c) The postman knocking at the door.
  (d) Somebody talking in his room.
  (e) A noise in his room.

10 How did Robert react?

  (a) He was astonished.
  (b) He greeted the newcomer.
  (c) He pulled a strange face.
  (d) He cried out in surprise.
  (e) He looked serious.

11 How had the journalist got in?

  (a) He had knocked and entered.
  (b) He had walked in through the open door.
  (c) He had unlocked the door.
  (d) He had slipped in when Georges went out.
  (e) He had come in with the caretaker.

12 Robert intended to deal with the journalist by

  (a) throwing him out.
  (b) seizing him by the ear.
  (c) throwing a pillow at him.
  (d) grabbing his arm.
  (e) throwing him to the floor with a pillow over his face.

Essay writing

This section deals with the main essay tests set by Boards: stories based on pictures, stories based on an outline or continuation of an outline, letters, more general essays, reproduction essays.

General advice

1 Read carefully all instructions about the number of words, special tenses to be used and any special viewpoint to be taken (e.g. are you meant to be one of the characters in the story?).
2 Plan your essay before you start to write.
3 List your paragraph headings and jot down some key sentences or notes *in French* for each paragraph.
4 By adding in more details build your outline into a rough copy. Check for mistakes and look for ways to improve this version.
5 Then, and only then, write up a neat copy.
6 Only write what you are confident you can handle. Some useful constructions for essays are given in the grammar reference, pp42–3, but if you are doubtful don't use them.
7 Above all else, check methodically, going through your work making separate checks for

    (a) verbs agreeing with subject
    (b) correct tense for the meaning and correct ending for that tense
    (c) adjectives in the right position (generally after the noun) and agreeing in gender and number with nouns or pronouns.
    (d) correct use of le/la/les, du/de la/des, etc (e.g. no mistakes like des bonbon*n*).

8 Practise in timed conditions before the examination until you can adjust your pace of work to allow for all these different stages.

Histoires illustrées (stories based on pictures)

1 Look at all the pictures several times, so you have the overall content clear in your mind. Imagine you are going to relate what happened to someone who hasn't seen the pictures or the title.
2 Look at each picture in turn and jot down *in French* the vocabulary and phrases that you know which fit the picture. Do not write anything in English in your notes.
3 Begin to build up your full version by adding one or two details to the bare bones. Can you answer in French questions like: how? who? when? why? what type?

4 If you are using past tenses, the following time phrases would be useful:

l'année dernière	last year	il y a deux mois	two months ago
l'été dernier	last summer	il y a une semaine	one week ago
la semaine dernière	last week	récemment	recently
mardi dernier	last Tuesday	il y a longtemps	a long time ago
il y a trois ans	three years ago		

5 The following phrases might help to link paragraphs

plus tard later
quelques heures plus tard a few hours later
au bout de quelques minutes after a few minutes
puis then ensuite next à ce moment-là at that moment
soudain suddenly tout d'un coup all at once
tout de suite straightaway

6 When writing up your neat copy think especially about past tenses; Use the imperfect for describing what things, people and places *were like* (e.g. what the weather *was* like, what sort of mood someone *was* in). Use the perfect to write down what event or step in the action *took place* at a particular moment.

7 *Check, check, check!* Can you write out from memory the check-list printed on p138?

Story based on outline

1 You are given a summary of a story in French which you have to expand into a full essay. Copy out the outline on to your rough paper with big gaps between each phrase. Work out the overall meaning of the story, thinking as you go along how you might expand on the bare details.

2 Build up your rough copy by writing in French in the gaps all the vocabulary you know which fits in with the meaning. Work on the same lines as for the picture essay, remembering that your finished version should make sense to someone who hasn't seen the outline.

3 *Check, check, check!* Make certain you haven't mis-spelt any words given to you in the outline.

Sample titles

1 Une famille écossaise passe des vacances dans une caravane en France. A Paris le père ne trouve plus les passeports. Il va au

commissariat de police. Un gendarme les a trouvés. La famille continue son voyage.   150 to 200 words. Use past tenses.   (SCE)

2 Nouvelle voiture – première excursion – où? quand? avec qui? – panne – conversation – pas d'essence – que faire?   100 words. Use past tenses.   (AEB)

3 A l'insu de (= unknown to) vos parents vous empruntez la voiture familiale. Au cours de la promenade il vous arrive un accident de sorte que vous ne rentrez chez vous que très tard. Décrivez l'incident et la scène de famille qui en résulte. A Le départ: les préparatifs; le but du voyage; la route; vos raisons de choisir ce moyen de transport. B L'accident et ses suites: l'endroit; la cause; le nombre de blessés; les dommages; les décisions prises. C Le retour: comment rentrez-vous? la réaction de vos parents; comment se termine l'incident?   180 to 200 words. Use past tenses.   (WJE)

Short story or continuation from an outline

1 In this type of essay you are given a few details to start off your story, but basically you have to think up the plot yourself.

2 Keep your plot simple and within the limitations of your French. Change your plot if you feel it is getting beyond your ability to express it in French.

3 As already suggested, build up an outline of key phrases in French, expanding on this outline as you work towards your final version.

4 Check, as always!

Sample titles

1 Le jeune Thomas était membre d'un groupe de son école qui voyageait en France en autocar. Arrivé à Lyon, pendant qu'on visitait les monuments de la ville, il s'est trouvé soudain seul. Un peu plus tard, il a découvert que l'autocar n'était plus dans le parking . . . Continue the story in about 150 words.   (OX)

2 Vous êtes touriste. Racontez un incident qui vous est arrivé lorsque vous étiez dans un port étranger.   140 to 150 words. Use past tenses.   (JMB)

3 One night you are awakened by a smell of smoke. You lie awake for some time wondering what it can be. Is it a fire or mother's cooking? Or is there some other explanation? Finally you put on your dressing-gown and go downstairs to investigate. Tell the whole story of what happened and how the incident ended.   130 to 150 words.   (CAM)

Letter writing

1 Some Boards give you a theme for your letter, others print a letter to which you must reply.

2 If there is a letter to read, study it very closely, paying special attention to the tenses used and any questions which are asked in different tenses (e.g. what *will* you do? as opposed to what *do* you do? or what *did* you do?). If the letter is written by a friend you will need to use *tu* in your answer, not *vous*.

3 For a good mark your letter must be
   (a) full (tick off on the question paper each point or reply you are supposed to make in your letter)
   (b) reasonably organized (build up from an outline as suggested, trying to link your paragraphs)
   (c) accurate (can you recite the check-list on p138?).

4 The layout for beginning and ending an informal letter should be as follows. What do you notice about the address and the position of the opening greeting on the page?

Banbury, le 14 juillet 1979

Cher Robert (or Chère Michelle)

Merci de ta lettre du premier juillet . . .

Meilleures pensées à toute ta famille.

Amitiés,
Jane

A more formal letter would start *Monsieur*, (*Madame* etc) and perhaps end *Salutations distinguées*, the rough equivalent of *Yours sincerely*.

1 Mon cher Michel,
   Je t'écris en toute hâte, parce que Jeannine veut sortir. C'est simplement pour te demander si tu pourras venir chez nous samedi prochain, et si tu pourras apporter ton électrophone et aussi des disques. Est-ce que tu amèneras ton amie? Nous serons contents de faire sa connaissance (surtout moi – tes amies sont toujours belles!).

   A propos, est-ce que tu as pu réparer la voiture? Qu'est-ce qu'elle avait?

   A bientôt,
   Pierre

Reply in about 100 words. (AEB)

2 Write in French a letter of application for a scholarship offered by an international youth organization, enabling young people to travel abroad. You must write not *less* than 140 and *not more than* 150 words giving *all* the information requested in the following extract from their regulations:

RENCONTRE DES JEUNES
Bourses de Voyage 1979

Les candidats sont priés de fournir les renseignements suivants:

1 Détails personnels (âge, domicile, éducation)
2 Intérêts particuliers (sports, loisirs)
3 Connaissance de langues étrangères
4 Voyages déjà entrepris à l'étranger
5 Choix de pays – raisons
6 Carrière future possible
7 Raison pour laquelle ce voyage est important.

(LOND)

3 It is the beginning of January. Write a letter, *in French*, to your correspondent in France thanking him (her) for his (her) card and telling him (her) how you spent your Christmas holidays.   150 to 200 words.   (SCE)

More general titles, discussions or descriptions
1 Choose a title which you can write well on *in French*, not a title which you know a lot about and could write on in English but know none of the vocabulary in the foreign language!
2 The routine of building up from a French outline, trying to link the arguments logically, should be a familiar one by now.
3 Accuracy in checking is still the key to success. However brilliant the arguments, you are wasting your time if the French is inaccurate.

Sample titles
1 Vous avez reçu la visite d'un étranger (ou d'une étrangère) venu(e) d'un pays tout à fait différent du vôtre. Racontez ce que vous avez fait pour lui faire connaître votre pays, votre façon de vivre, vos coutumes etc.   120 to 130 words.   (LOND)
2 Faites la description d'une ville française ou anglaise que vous connaissez.

3 Une visite au marché OU à un musée.
4 Une conversation avec un(e) ami(e) au sujet des vacances de Noël.
   Numbers 2–4: about 150 words.   (SU)

Reproduction essays

1 In this test you normally hear a short story twice and then have to
   write down what happened in your own words with the help of a
   printed summary which is provided.
2 Read any instructions about what tenses to use. Normally you will
   be using the imperfect and perfect as in a picture essay (p139).
3 Use the outline to help you, but do not mis-copy any of the words
   given. Verbs are generally in the present tense or infinitive, so you
   must put them into the correct tense for the story yourself.
4 The number of words you are allowed to use is limited, so concentrate
   on getting in the main points of the action, rather than waste words
   adding in any extra inventions yourself, as you might do in a picture
   essay.
5 Good answers must be full (including all the key events) and accurate.
   The need for checking should be obvious by now, and you ought to
   be able to reel off the standard check-list.

Test passage

Do not read this passage yourself. You will have to ask someone to read
it to you twice when you want to attempt the test, the first time at
normal speed, followed by a second reading somewhat more slowly.
Your *assistant* can do this 'live' or make two recordings on cassette.
Follow the procedure below:

1 Copy this summary of the story on to a separate piece of paper. *No
   defects!*: Angélique – enfants inadaptés – Christophe lisait très mal –
   visite du médecin – défauts – les notes dans le cahier.
2 Keeping the outline in front of you, but making no notes, listen to
   the two readings of the story. After the second reading you have
   about one hour in which to write down the story in your own
   words. Use past tenses and write between 150–160 words.

No defects!

Mademoiselle Angélique Dubois enseignait dans une école pour les
enfants inadaptés. Les élèves étaient souvent charmants et fort intelligents, mais à cause de maladies ou de malheurs domestiques ils

avaient fait très peu de progrès dans leurs études. Ils avaient donc grand besoin d'attention et d'encouragement.

Angélique aimait surtout Christophe, un garçon de sept ans, énergique et doué. Quand il était tout petit, une maladie l'avait empêché d'aller à l'école pendant une année entière. Il lisait donc très mal à ce moment-là, malgré son intelligence.

Un jour, Angélique dut annoncer à sa classe la visite du médecin qui venait tous les six mois s'assurer de la santé des enfants. Elle remarqua que le petit Christophe était devenu tout pâle à l'idée même d'une visite médicale.

Mais il n'y avait rien à faire, et le lendemain Christophe passa à son tour dans la pièce qu'on avait réservée au médecin. Vingt minutes plus tard il en sortit, le visage rayonnant de bonheur, et il courut tout de suite chercher Angélique.

– Tout va bien! il est content de moi! s'écria-t-il. J'ai seulement des défauts!

– Des défauts? Qu'est-ce que tu veux dire, mon enfant?

– Oui, des défauts. J'ai vu le médecin écrire quelque chose dans son cahier sous le titre 'défauts'.

Angélique, inquiétée, alla tout raconter au médecin. Il l'écouta jusqu'au bout, puis éclata de rire. Sans dire un mot il ouvrit son cahier et lui montra ses notes. Sous le titre 'défauts' il y avait un seul mot: 'rien'! (o&c)

Pictures for essay practice

The next three left-hand pages contain pictures for essay practice. Although it would be more natural to write about the pictures in the present tense (saying what is going on), write instead in *past tenses*, saying what *happened*, what *was happening* or what people or places *were* like, since this is what you are asked to do in the O level picture essay in most cases. Follow these steps.

1 Make sure you have read and understood the notes on pp138–9 about how to tackle picture essays.
2 Make sure you revise the vocabulary areas relevant to the picture you are going to work on. Vocabulary unit numbers are given for your reference overpage.
3 Work on one picture at a time, covering over the opposite right-hand page.
4 Write as much as you can about the picture, using all the techniques explained to you, including the checking procedures.

5 When you have finished your version, try and find someone competent to go over your work with you. The right-hand pages give you some idea of how you might have tackled the pictures, starting with a list of useful words, followed by suggestions as to how those words could be built up into full sentences. Many of the sentences go 'beyond' the picture and suggest additional ideas.

6 Practise writing on pictures as much as possible. For a start you could try the six pictures in the oral section on pp156–60.

Vocabulary units to revise

Picture 1 Units 15 and 20
Picture 2 Units 7, 18 and 22
Picture 3 Units 7, 18, 19, 21 and 22
Picture 4 Units 4 and 20
Picture 5 Unit 19
Picture 6 Units 2, 3, 5 and 6

1

faire une sortie à la campagne – variété de paysages – s'arrêter – crevaison – téléphoner au touring-secours – en pleine campagne – remplacer le pneu crevé – s'amuser à – passer un moment agréable – pneu de rechange.

La semaine dernière la famille Delage a décidé de faire une sortie à la campagne. Quelle variété de paysages! Des lacs, des forêts, des montagnes! Malheureusement, après plusieurs heures de voyage ils ont dû s'arrêter à cause d'une crevaison. M. Delage voulait téléphoner au touring-secours, mais ils étaient en pleine campagne, à plusieurs kilomètres du village le plus proche. 'Tu peux remplacer le pneu crevé toi-même, chéri?' a dit sa femme. 'Je vais essayer,' a-t-il répondu. Ses deux enfants se sont amusés à jouer avec un ballon. Les deux chiens, aussi, ont passé un moment agréable à jouer ensemble. Leur maître a dû travailler dur pour mettre le pneu de rechange.

2

faire du camping – apporter – tente – duvets – lits de camp – dresser – commencer à – préparer le repas – réchaud à gaz – à table – mère de famille – pas un seul nuage – jouer à – s'amuser à – boisson froide – sortir de – voler des saucisses – être en train de.

L'été dernier les Bouvreuil ont fait du camping en Normandie. Ils ont apporté beaucoup de choses dans le coffre de leur voiture – une tente, des duvets et des lits de camp. Quand ils sont arrivés au camping, M. Bouvreuil a dû dresser la tente et les deux enfants l'ont aidé. Mme Bouvreuil a commencé à préparer le repas sur un petit réchaud à gaz. 'A table!' a-t-elle crié quand le repas était prêt. Il était midi. Le soleil brillait et il n'y avait pas un seul nuage au ciel. Des jeunes gens jouaient au badminton et une jeune fille s'amusait à lire un livre, une boisson froide à sa main gauche. Soudain, une mère de famille est sortie d'une tente, très fâchée. Deux chiens avaient volé des saucisses et maintenant ils étaient en train de les manger!

3

passer des vacances d'été – hôtel de luxe – côte ouest – remplir des fiches de voyageur – tout près de – se baigner – passer plusieurs heures à – faire doux – prendre un bain de soleil – jouer à – installé à.

Il y a trois ans M. et Mme Esch ont passé leurs vacances d'été dans un grand hôtel de luxe sur la côte ouest. Quand ils sont arrivés, ils sont allés tout de suite à la réception pour remplir des fiches de voyageur. 'Qu'est-ce qu'on va faire cet après-midi?' a demandé M. Esch à sa femme. 'Nous sommes tout près de la plage, mais je préfère me baigner dans la piscine de l'hôtel,' a-t-elle répondu. Cet après-midi, Mme Esch a passé plusieurs heures à se baigner. Il faisait très doux. Une jeune fille prenait un bain de soleil à côté de la piscine, des jeunes gens jouaient au tennis et un monsieur était installé à une table sur la terrasse, un verre de limonade et un bol de fruits devant lui.

4

faire une sortie à la campagne – se lever tôt – faire les préparatifs – après avoir – charger – coffre – partir de bonne heure – prendre un panier-repas – en pleine campagne – plat principal – faire une promenade – en fin d'après-midi – ranger – avant de.

Il y a deux semaines la famille Vié a décidé de faire une sortie à la campagne. Ils se sont levés tôt pour faire tous les préparatifs et ils sont partis de bonne heure, après avoir chargé le coffre de leur voiture de toutes les provisions. Ils ont pris leur panier-repas en pleine campagne. Ils ont mangé des tartines avec du fromage. 'Veux-tu me passer la bouteille de vin rouge, chérie?' a demandé M. Vié. 'Bien sûr,' a répondu sa femme. 'Et les enfants? Vous en voulez aussi?' – 'Non, merci, maman,' ont-ils répondu. Leur chien a pris un os comme plat principal! Après avoir mangé, ils ont fait une promenade ensemble. En fin d'après-midi ils ont rangé toutes leurs affaires dans le coffre de leur voiture, avant de rentrer chez eux.

5

passer une quinzaine – côte atlantique – séjour – passer la matinée à – prendre un bain de soleil – se bronzer – acheter à – marchand de glaces – choix de parfums – avant de – faire des châteaux de sable – se baigner – faire de la voile – s'amuser bien.

Juillet dernier nous avons passé une quinzaine au bord de la mer, sur la côte atlantique. Le premier jour de notre séjour nous sommes allés tout de suite à la plage. Mes parents ont passé la matinée à prendre un bain de soleil. Ils se sont bronzés très rapidement, car il faisait très chaud ce jour-là. Nous avons acheté des glaces au marchand (il y avait un grand choix de parfums) avant de faire des châteaux de sable. Il faisait un temps merveilleux – quelques gens en maillot de bain se baignaient dans la mer, d'autres faisaient de la voile. Même des chiens s'amusaient bien dans l'eau.

6

passer la soirée – avoir envie de – le journal de huit heures – passer à l'écran – ennuyer – jouer aux cartes – romans policiers – aîné – s'intéresser à – plutôt – bavarder – venir de – pendant que – s'amuser à – pantoufle.

Hier soir je n'avais pas envie de sortir – j'ai passé toute la soirée chez moi dans le salon. Tout d'abord j'ai regardé le journal de huit heures à la télévision, mais, après, un western est passé à l'écran qui m'ennuyait beaucoup. J'ai décidé de jouer aux cartes. 'Christine, tu veux jouer aussi?' ai-je demandé à ma sœur. 'Ah non,' a-t-elle répondu, 'je préfère lire, merci.' Les romans policiers lui plaisaient beaucoup. Mon frère aîné, assis sur le canapé, s'intéressait aussi à son livre, plutôt qu'à la télévision. Ma sœur aînée bavardait avec son ami, qui venait de lire le journal, pendant que notre chien s'amusait à manger une pantoufle.

Oral tests

There is a limit to the amount of help a book can give you in coping with oral tests. Oral practice can only be had by talking! The language laboratory, or recordings on disc and cassette can improve your accent. Listening to the high-speed French on French stations on long-wave radio, or on the language programmes on British radio or television, can also help to improve intonation and accent, regardless of how little you actually understand. Oral fluency has to be built up gradually, by conversation practice with your teacher or someone else. You cannot suddenly become fluent just before the exam, however hard you might work at it. The oral examination is usually some time *before* the written papers, by the way.

The following sections deal with the main types of oral test. At the end of the section there are some pictures to work on.

Reading aloud a prepared passage

Use your preparation time to work out the general meaning of the passage, as well as preparing yourself to pronounce the words correctly. You are normally given marks for a good accent (i.e. pronunciation and intonation, the way in which your voice goes up and down) and for fluency of expression (i.e. do you sound as though you understand what you are reading?).

Set questions on a picture

Your teacher, or the examiner, has a set of printed questions. Normally it is not permissible for the question to be altered or rephrased by the examiner, nor are you allowed to see the picture beforehand. The fluency, accuracy and intelligibility of your reply is assessed, rather than your accent. In other words, do you reply reasonably quickly and smoothly, without mistakes of grammar and in a way which a French person would understand?

Listen carefully to the question you are asked, but don't repeat bits of it without thinking. The questions are often designed to test the ease with which you can manipulate the language by changing something like a verb or a pronoun. Study the table of typical mistakes below: most of these are the result of nerves, so do try and keep calm!

Question	Wrong reply	Mistake	Correct reply
Tu aimes nager?	Oui, tu aimes nager.	wrong person	J'aime nager.
Tu y es allé avec ta famille?	Oui, j'y suis allé avec ta famille.	wrong pronoun	J'y suis allé avec ma famille.
Qu'est-ce qu'il a fait?	Il a fait quitter la salle.	wrongly repeating *fait*	Il a quitté la salle.
Qu'est-ce que votre père a comme voiture?	Il a comme voiture Renault 12.	wrongly repeating part of question	Il a une Renault 12.
Vous regardez souvent la télé?	Oui, je regarder souvent.	wrong ending on verb; no word for *it*	Oui, je la regarde souvent.
Qu'est-ce que tu ferais à sa place?	Je téléphone à la police.	wrong tense	Je téléphon- erais à la police.
Où vas-tu passer tes vacances cet été?	J'ai passé deux semaines en France.	wrong tense	Je vais passer deux semaines en France.
Tu joues au tennis en été?	Oui, j'ai joué au tennis en été.	wrong tense	Oui, je joue au tennis en été

Make your answers interesting; use pronouns *if* you are confident you can handle them. *But* above all else, try and be accurate with verbs and tenses.

Role playing

You are generally given a card with instructions in English about the things you are to say in French. In your preparation time, think carefully about how to put the phrases into correct French, rather than translating word for word from English. Think about what the examiner will be listening for in your answers; is it a particular tense or structure?

When you give your answers, the examiner will play a role too (e.g. he may be the shopkeeper and you the shopper). This means that you may be asked extra questions to see if you react when given a choice or if you understand some new piece of information or changed circumstances. The role playing should develop like a real conversation, so listen to what is said to you and react accordingly.

Talking about a picture

If you are given time to prepare, approach this test rather as you would tackle the essay paper, as explained on pp138–9. Think in French: what are the phrases and vocabulary which you know which tie in with the picture? Build up complete sentences from your key phrases. This is preferable to thinking in English, trying to translate and getting halfway through a sentence and discovering you don't know how to finish it in French.

Be as accurate as you can in your use of verbs. If you are asked to say what is going on, you must use the present tense, using *venir de* + *infinitive* to describe what someone has just done.

General conversation

This may be developed from a picture or it may be everyday chat.

A conversation is two-sided, so you mustn't make a long, prepared, uninterrupted speech. Respond to the questions that the examiner chips in. Don't be afraid of altering the direction of the conversation by asking the examiner a question if you feel this might help you.

However, just because you mustn't make a speech doesn't mean that you cannot prepare at all for this test. It is not difficult to work out in advance the sort of things you might be asked. They will be mostly everyday questions which a naturally curious host would put to you if you were on a visit to a French family – your own background; members of your family; their ages and occupations; your home and who does what at home; your daily routine at home and school; your career ambitions; your town or village and its facilities; travel and holidays in this country and abroad; your hobbies and sports. Be prepared to answer questions on all these topics. The vocabulary section in this book should be one source of help in this.

Prepared topics and questions

Some Boards publish – before the exam – a list of topics on which you should prepare a short talk, or a list of questions from which some questions will be drawn in the examination. Take advantage of this by polishing up your answers over a period of many months, not just weeks, before the oral test. The French *assistant(e)* in the school may practise the questions with you. Write your talk by putting together phrases which you know to be correct French, rather than translating a talk from English into French. Recording your talk on cassette, playing it back and re-recording several times, may help to improve the fluency, or flow, of your performance.

Pictures for oral practice

The next three left-hand pages contain pictures for oral practice. Follow these steps.

1 Make sure you have read and understood all the hints on oral practice on pp152–3.
2 Make sure you revise the vocabulary themes which are relevant to the picture you are going to work on. Vocabulary unit numbers are given for reference at the foot of this page.
3 Work on one picture at a time, starting with the right-hand page covered.
4 Look briefly at the picture, then uncover, one at a time, the set questions on each drawing. Answer out loud in French as you uncover each question. Possible answers to these set questions are given in the answer section right at the back of the book.
5 Now study the picture in more detail and try talking about it out loud, using the present tense.
6 Uncover the general questions printed beneath the set questions on each picture. Give your own answer. There are no answers printed to these questions, as the replies vary so much from individual to individual. Try and imagine extra conversational questions which might crop up and work out your replies to them.
7 For extra practice, use the pictures in the essay section on pp146–50. Try and work out what the set questions and conversational questions to those pictures might be.

Vocabulary units to revise

Picture 1 Units 13 and 14
Picture 2 Units 9 and 10
Picture 3 Units 17, 22, 23 and 26

Picture 4 Units 2, 3, 4 and 27
Picture 5 Unit 4
Picture 6 Units 8, 13 and 27

A

1 Est-ce que ce train part de la gare?
2 Que feront les voyageurs dans quelques instants?
3 Pourquoi est-ce qu'il y a beaucoup de lettres par terre?

General questions

Expliquez ce que c'est une consigne.

Expliquez ce que c'est un buffet.

A la gare, où est-ce qu'on prend son billet normalement?

Quels préparatifs feriez-vous si vous deviez faire un voyage en chemin de fer?

Décrivez un voyage que vous avez fait en chemin de fer.

Quels sont les avantages et les inconvénients des voyages en chemin de fer?

Est-ce que vous préférez voyager en voiture ou en train? Pourquoi?

B

1 Combien d'argent est-ce que la dame doit payer?
2 Que fera la caissière si la dame lui donne 298.25?
3 Comment savez-vous que le magasin est un grand supermarché ou un hypermarché?

General questions

Que fait une caissière?

Est-ce que vous achetez vos disques/livres/chaussures dans un super-marché normalement? Pourquoi/pas?

Quels sont les avantages des supermarchés pour les ménagères? Et les inconvénients?

Est-ce que vous aidez votre mère à faire ses achats?

Faites la description d'un grand magasin que vous connaissez.

Vous faites les magasins avec cinquante livres en poche. Imaginez votre après-midi.

C

1 Est-ce que ces feuilles sont par terre depuis longtemps, pensez-vous?
2 Quel temps a-t-il fait pendant la nuit?
3 Que fera la jeune fille avec ces fleurs, pensez-vous?
4 Est-ce que ce jeune fermier a fini son travail?

General questions

Quelle saison préférez-vous? Pourquoi?
Pourquoi les Anglais parlent-ils toujours du temps?
Quels sports peut-on pratiquer quand il neige?
Quel genre de paysage aimez-vous? Pourquoi?
Qu'est-ce qu'on voit à la campagne au printemps?
Est-ce que vous aimez faire des sorties à la campagne? Pourquoi?
Est-ce que vous avez un chien? Qui est-ce qui le promène?
En quoi le rôle du fermier est-il important?
Quels changements ont eu lieu dans la vie des fermiers ces dernières années?
Est-ce que vous voudriez devenir fermier? Pourquoi/pas?

D

1 Pourquoi est-ce que le petit garçon à gauche sourit?
2 Qu'est-ce que la mère de famille est en train de faire?
3 Pourquoi est-ce que le père fait sortir le chien?

General questions

A quoi servent un réfrigérateur, une cuisinière et une machine à laver?
Comment pourriez-vous aider à la maison?
Qui fait le ménage chez vous?
Décrivez votre cuisine.
Que feriez-vous si vous cassiez une assiette dans la cuisine?
Qu'est-ce que vous avez fait ce matin entre sept et neuf heures?
Qu'est-ce qu'on fait chez vous le dimanche?

E

1 Est-ce que ces gens ont fini leur repas?
2 Que fera la dame à droite?
3 Pourquoi est-ce que le petit garçon quitte sa place?

General questions
Est-ce que vous aimez dîner dans un restaurant? Pourquoi/pas?
Décrivez brièvement un repas que vous avez pris un jour dans un restaurant.
Est-ce que vous avez jamais goûté la nourriture française? Cela vous a plu?
Quelle est la différence entre 'un menu à prix fixe' et un repas 'à la carte' dans un restaurant?
Quelles sont les heures des repas chez vous?
Qui est-ce qui prépare les repas chez vous?
Est-ce que vous avez un repas favori? Lequel?

F

1 Que faisait l'homme avant de tomber de l'échelle?
2 Que fera la voiture si la dame et son enfant traversent la rue au passage clouté?
3 Est-ce que le jeune garçon à gauche est allé en ville pour voir un film, pensez-vous?

General questions
Expliquez ce que c'est qu' un passage clouté.
Est-ce que vous aimez les villes? Pourquoi/pas?
Quels sont les problèmes d'un automobiliste dans une grande ville?
Quelles sont les principales distractions de votre ville/de la ville la plus proche?
Par quels moyens de transports est-elle desservie?
Décrivez le centre de votre ville/de la ville la plus proche.
Donnez quelques détails sur l'histoire de cette ville.
A votre avis, quels changements verra-t-on dans la ville d'ici vingt ans?

Dictation

Dictation is a very difficult test in French, but if you get depressed over your low scores it might be worth finding out how many marks the dictation test counts for in the examination you are taking. Lots of practice is necessary for a high mark, but concentrating on three main areas will definitely improve your performance:

* attention to grammar
* attention to sounds
* care in writing down and checking

Grammatical points

1 Before you write down a verb, find its subject, *je*, *tu*, *il* etc, and make sure you spell the ending correctly for that person in the particular tense.

2 Don't forget that the sound of the verb alone does not always make it clear whether the subject is singular or plural. Look out and listen for other clues. For example,

il finiss*ait son* travail   *he* was finishing *his* work
ils finiss*aient leur* travail   *they* were finishing *their* work

3 The spelling of the verb after *qui* depends on *who* or *what* is the *subject*.

*l'*employé qui travaille à la poste
les employés qui travaill*ent* à la poste

4 With *-er* verbs the infinitive *donner* (to give) and the past participle *donné* (given) sound the same. If there is a part of *être* or *avoir* coupled with an *-er* verb then you must be dealing with a sentence in the perfect tense:

je *suis* arrivé (I arrived); ils *ont* joué (they played)

If there is no part of *être* or *avoir*, then the second verb must be an infinitive:

je *sais* nag*er* (I can swim); il *voulait* chant*er* (he wanted to sing)

Be especially careful when *pouvoir, devoir, savoir, vouloir* are themselves in the perfect that you don't mis-spell the verb that follows:

il a pu ferm*er* le coffre (he managed *to close* the boot)
NOT il a pu ferm*é* le coffre (he managed clos*ed* the boot)

5 Words like *sans, pour, de, à, par* followed directly by a verb need the infinitive spelling of that verb:
sans parl*er*; *pour* arriv*er* à l'heure; il a fini *par* trouv*er* une place

6 Words like *everybody, the family, the group*, take a singular ending on the verb, even though more than one person is involved:
tout le monde *est* heureux; le groupe *était* parti; la famille *est* rentr*ée* à la maison.
la plupart (the majority) is the exception and takes a plural:
la plupart des élèves mang*ent* chez eux

7 Apply the general rule that verbs which use *être* to form *past tenses* take extra -*s*, -*e* or -*es* on the past participle; verbs that take avoir do not.

elle s'*est* habill*ée*   nous *sommes* arriv*és*
elle *a* crié   nous *avons* fini

8 When writing *adjectives*, make sure they *agree* in *gender* and *number* with the noun or pronoun to which they refer.

Sounds

With the help of your teacher make sure you are clear about the differences in pronunciation between the following pairs of words:

je finir*ai*	je finir*ais*
en ét*é*	il ét*ait*
le d*é*	d*ès*
et	est
ou	eu
roue	rue
vous	vu
tout	tu
sans	son
dans	dont
coussin	cousin
poisson	poison

Writing down and checking

1 During the first reading, when you do no writing, try and work out the general meaning of the passage, using the title to help you. Pay attention to the tenses used and the sex of the characters, as this will affect agreements of verbs and adjectives.

2 When the passage is read slowly in sections, write each phrase down *after* the person has finished speaking. The phrase will be repeated after you've written it down, so that you can check that you have missed nothing out.

3 On the third and final reading, after you've written down the entire passage, follow very carefully, checking your version word for word against what is read out.

4 In the last few minutes of revision, check systematically, rather than just read through, for the following points

* every verb agrees with its subject, with special attention to perfect tense endings
* every adjective agrees with its noun or pronoun
* every article agrees with its noun (des homm*es* not des homm*e*)

Make three separate checks, not one check looking for three things at once.

5 Try to understand what you are writing, rather than writing down a lot of disconnected sounds. There will be some new words which you will have to try and spell without ever having seen them in print, but concentrate on getting the words you think you know right. Trying to make some sense of what you are writing may well help you with the spelling of a word.

6 Write clearly, as you must do in all parts of the examination. Don't leave accents in a horizontal position (-), halfway between ` and ´; 'sitting on the fence' like this will cost you marks.

7 If punctuation is going to be dictated to you in French in your examination make sure your teacher gives you a written list of words in French to learn for full stop, comma, colon, question mark etc.

4 Answers to tests

Revising grammar

Forming the perfect tense of être verbs (p16)
1 Le prince Charles est né en 1945. 2 Elle est montée sur son vélo.
3 Je suis parti de Paris il y a un an. 4 Les deux jeunes filles sont
allées en France. 5 Les deux agents sont descendus du train. 6 Le
voleur est sorti du supermarché. 7 Je suis resté à la maison. 8 Les
deux soldats sont entrés dans la caserne.

The perfect tense of reflexive verbs (p17)
1 Ils se sont réveillés à sept heures et demie ce matin-là. 2 Mme
Janvier s'est levée tout de suite. 3 Puis elle s'est lavée. 4 Il s'est
habillé en écoutant sa femme. 5 L'homme s'est rasé à la hâte. 6 Les
deux jeunes filles se sont dépêchées d'arriver à huit heures. 7 Je me
suis reposé ce matin-là. 8 Les enfants se sont couchés à minuit. 9 Les
deux jeunes filles se sont sauvées quand elles ont vu l'homme dans le
parc.

The perfect tense of avoir verbs (p18)
1 Ils ont mangé leurs sandwiches. 2 J'ai téléphoné à mon père.
3 Elle a couru à la gendarmerie. 4 J'ai bu une tasse de café. 5 Ils
ont dû quitter l'hôtel. 6 Il a fini son travail. 7 Le professeur a puni
les deux élèves. 8 Le garçon a rempli le verre. 9 Elle a acheté un
cadeau. 10 Il a dormi pendant huit heures. 11 Ils ont dit au revoir à
leur père. 12 Les deux garçons ont disparu. 13 Il a écrit son nom et
son adresse. 14 Il a perdu son portefeuille. 15 Ils ont vendu leur
maison. 16 J'ai entendu un bruit. 17 L'élève a fait une erreur dans
son devoir. 18 Leur mère a lu la carte postale. 19 Ils ont mis le
panier dans le coffre de la voiture. 20 Elle a ouvert la fenêtre. 21 Elle
a offert un pourboire. 22 Il a plu mercredi dernier. 23 J'ai pu me
sauver. 24 Il a pris son parapluie. 25 Il a suivi le voleur. 26 J'ai vu
le film à la télévision. 27 Leur mère a conduit la voiture à la gare.
28 La jeune fille a reçu une récompense. 29 Il a écouté la radio
pendant une demi-heure. 30 Ils ont trouvé une boîte dans le grenier.

Être verbs which sometimes take avoir (p19)

1 Je suis sorti à minuit.   **2** Il est passé devant la gare routière.   **3** Elle est montée sur sa moto.   **4** Il a descendu sa serviette.   **5** Je lui ai passé la bouteille.   **6** Ils sont descendus.   **7** Nous sommes sortis de l'église.   **8** Il a sorti son bic.   **9** Il a monté les marches.   **10** Ils sont montés.

The imperfect tense (p20)

1 J'habitais Birmingham.   **2** Elle était fatiguée après le voyage.
3 L'appartement était vide.   **4** Il tenait un revolver à la main.   **5** Elle portait des souliers noirs.   **6** Ils écoutaient la radio quand ils ont entendu un bruit.   **7** Ils avaient faim.   **8** Le garçon était content de sa récompense.   **9** Il se couchait toujours à dix heures.   **10** Ils se sauvaient quand la police est arrivée.

The pluperfect tense (p20)

1 We had returned home in good time.   **2** I had chosen a blue dress.
3 He had already seen the film.   **4** They had arrived before me.
5 Had you forgotten your umbrella?

Recognition of the past historic (p21)

1 She left at midnight.   **2** They worked all day.   **3** He drank his coffee.   **4** They went to the pub.   **5** 'Hullo,' he said to me.   **6** She came to see him that evening.   **7** They took this decision.   **8** It rained that night.   **9** They died after the battle.   **10** It was necessary to leave without further delay (in context, translate as: I had to, we had to etc, rather than use 'necessary').   **11** He ate a slice of bread.   **12** They had to demolish the house.   **13** She wrote a letter to him.   **14** All at once they were frightened.   **15** She managed to escape.

The future tense (p22)

1 It will be necessary (in context: I will have to, you will have to etc) to leave straightaway.   **2** He'll send me a postcard.   **3** They will come round at about six o'clock.   **4** You'll be able to come with me.   **5** She'll want to have a wash before having dinner.   **6** You will have to set out very early.   **7** I'll go there all on my own.   **8** She'll be pleased to see me.   **9** We'll have a lot to do tomorrow morning.   **10** What will you do after the summer holidays?   **11** J'aurai seize ans en juin.   **12** Je serai triste de quitter l'école.   **13** Je pourrai aller en France l'année prochaine.   **14** Nous serons à Paris dans huit jours.   **15** Mon frère ira à Paris l'année prochaine.

The conditional tense (p23)

1 Mum said she would be back before six. **2** He would make a fortune if he went to the USA. **3** I would be pleased to see her again. **4** I wouldn't know what to do. **5** I'd go to Switzerland, if I had enough money. **6** If I were in your position, I wouldn't drink that fifth glass of red wine. **7** They had explained that they would arrive a bit late. **8** I told him (her) that I would send him (her) a letter. **9** I'd be frightened if I went there on my own. **10** He told us he would see us the following day. **11** je ferais une croisière **12** je prendrais le petit déjeuner au lit **13** j'irais au Canada **14** je boirais du champagne **15** je conduirais une Rolls **16** je ne travaillerais plus **17** j'offrirais des pourboires de cinquante francs **18** je voyagerais en Concorde **19** je mangerais dans des restaurants chics **20** je serais plus heureux, peut-être!

The present tense (p24)

1 Ils mettent les valises dans la voiture. **2** Nous buvons du thé au petit déjeuner. **3** Vous devez partir tout de suite, mes amis. **4** Oui, je connais bien Paris. **5** Vous prenez du sucre, monsieur? **6** Elle vient demain. **7** Je lis un roman policier. **8** Le train part à huit heures. **9** Ils font fortune. **10** Nous écrivons beaucoup en français. **11** Je sors ce soir. **12** Je peux vous voir demain. **13** Ma mère me conduit à l'école. **14** Je sais que j'ai raison. **15** Ils vont au match samedi.

How well do you know all your tenses? (p24)

1 I would drink another glass, if I weren't driving. **2** They were running towards the exit. **3** I'm reading the newspaper. **4** We will ski in the Alps. **5** Are you coming? **6** He had seen me the week before. **7** He took out his biro. **8** The children are putting the groceries in the car. **9** I would like to go to China. **10** He was leaving the house when the police arrived. **11** The soldiers came to his aid. **12** He was amazed. **13** He was holding a revolver in his hand. **14** She became famous. **15** The two women finished their meal and left the room. **16** La famille est arrivée en France. **17** J'ouvrais la porte quand le téléphone a sonné. **18** Je bois une tasse de café à huit heures du matin. **19** Il portait une veste verte. **20** Il a lu la lettre et a écrit une réponse. **21** On dit qu'ils sont riches. **22** Je vais faire les lits. **23** Il a offert un pourboire à l'employé. **24** Je fais mes devoirs. **25** Elle s'est levée à six heures. **26** Il a mis les livres sur la table. **27** Il pleuvait et le ciel était noir. **28** Elle sera contente. **29** Ils ont conduit à la gare. **30** Ils allaient à la gare quand ils ont vu le voleur.

Devoir (p25)

1 I used to have to go to school on foot when we had no car.   **2** They ought to respect their parents.   **3** They found no sign of him – he must have escaped.   **4** I have to leave you now.   **5** I had to go home immediately.

Pouvoir (p26)

1 When I was twenty-five I could go to bed late and get up early.
2 You may step into the manager's office now.   **3** He might arrive tomorrow.   **4** I didn't manage to repair the car.   **5** Would you be able to do this type of work?

Vouloir (p26)

1 Would you mind passing me the salt?   **2** When he saw his wife, M. Legrand insisted on sending for the doctor straightaway.   **3** After long days of work she wanted to go to bed early.   **4** They would like to go on a cruise.   **5** Do you mind putting your things away?

Avoir (p27)

1 Ils ont raison.   **2** Vous avez tort, messieurs.   **3** Il avait mal au pied.
4 Elle avait dix-huit ans.   **5** Tu as soif?   **6** Ils avaient faim.   **7** J'ai besoin d'argent.   **8** Elle avait chaud.   **9** Tu as froid?   **10** Paul avait peur de son professeur.

Faire (p27)

1 Mme Cottard faisait les achats au supermarché.   **2** Il faisait la vaisselle quand sa femme est arrivée.   **3** J'ai fait un séjour de trois semaines en France.   **4** Nous allons faire une promenade cet après-midi.   **5** Papa fait le ménage chez nous.   **6** Nous faisions un séjour en Allemagne quand l'accident est arrivé.   **7** Ils ont fait une excursion en voiture.   **8** C'est moi qui fais la cuisine quand nous faisons du camping.   **9** On va faire une promenade?   **10** Mark et Sandra allaient faire la vaisselle mais ils étaient trop fatigués.

Aller, entendre, voir, aimer, préférer (p28)

1 Ils ont vu le voleur quitter le magasin.   **2** J'ai entendu le cambrioleur entrer dans le salon.   **3** Il allait pleuvoir.   **4** Tu aimes regarder la télé?   **5** Nous préférions dîner chez nous.

Aider à, commencer à, continuer à, réussir à, passer (heures) à (p28)

1 Je passe deux heures tous les soirs à écouter mon transistor.   **2** Il a commencé à pleuvoir.   **3** L'agent a réussi à arrêter le voleur.   **4** Il a continué à lire son livre.   **5** J'aidais Papa à laver la voiture quand il est arrivé.

Décider de, essayer de, cesser de, refuser de, oublier de (p29)

1 Il a cessé de neiger.   2 Ils ont décidé de manger au restaurant.
3 Il essayait de parler allemand.   4 L'homme a refusé de partir.   5 Il avait oublié de faire ses devoirs.

Demander à . . . de, dire à . . . de, défendre à . . . de, permettre à . . . de (p29)

1 He had told us to park the car in front of the block.   2 The farmer had forbidden them to go into the field.   3 The father didn't use to allow his daughter to come home late.   4 I asked the policeman to help us.   5 They had told him to bring an umbrella.

Articles (p30)

1 J'ai vu les deux hommes dans le café.   2 Il y avait des femmes dans la voiture.   3 J'aime les biscuits.   4 D'habitude je prends du fromage au lieu d'un dessert.   5 Vous avez du vin rouge?   6 Il y a des mouches dans mon potage.   7 Voulez-vous des frites ou des pommes de terre?
8 Je déteste les livres.

Negatives (p31)

1 Elle n'a rien mangé.   2 Je ne fume pas.   3 Nous ne nous sommes pas dépêchés.   4 L'agent n'a vu personne.   5 Il ne boit plus.
6 Personne ne par ait.   7 Il n'a bu qu'un litre de bière.

Negatives (p31)

1 Je n'ai pas d'amis.   2 Il n'y a pas de douche.   3 Je n'ai plus d'appétit.   4 On n'a plus de verres dans le café.   5 Il n'y a pas de place.   6 Je n'ai pas de chocolat.

Interrogatives (p33)

1 'Comment est ta voiture?' a demandé Nicole.   2 Il a dit, 'Au revoir.'   3 'Bonjour,' a-t-il dit.   4 'Pourquoi?' a demandé l'agent.
5 'Au secours!' ont crié les enfants.

Adjectives (p34)

1 heureuses   2 chère   3 neuves   4 naturelle   5 favorite

Position of adjectives (p34)

1 He's one of my ex-pupils.   2 He's a dear colleague.   3 It's my own room.   4 Do you have a clean shirt?   5 It's a very old school.   6 He's a good chap.   7 Is it an expensive watch?   8 Poor (old) lady!
9 She's a very hard-up lady.

Comparisons (p35)

1 That's less expensive. **2** He is as ambitious as his father. **3** I find this wine is bad; that one is better. **4** The film we saw on the telly was worse. **5** She is prettier than her mother.

Superlatives (p35)

1 It's the largest hotel in Paris. **2** Fawlty Towers is the worst hotel in England. **3** It's the best restaurant in France. **4** I live in the tallest block of flats in the town. **5** He's the most intelligent person in our family. **6** It's the least visited monument in the region.

Adverbs (p36)

1 That happens rarely. **2** They often eat at the restaurant. **3** You've finished quickly! **4** You came home late last night. **5** He writes better in French than his sister. **6** He plays well. **7** You read badly. **8** Never mind! **9** So much the better! **10** Describe exactly what you saw. **11** Obviously you are right. **12** He is fairly intelligent.

Expressions of quantity (p37)

1 trop de bière **2** assez d'intelligence **3** deux kilos de pommes **4** deux cent cinquante grammes de bonbons **5** une bouteille d'eau **6** un paquet de thé **7** un peu d'argent **8** beaucoup d'amis **9** un verre de vin rouge **10** deux litres de lait.

Prepositions – A, au, à la, à l', aux (p37)

1 La voiture était à dix kilomètres du village. **2** à soixante kilomètres à l'heure. **3** Il joue au tennis. **4** Je pensais à mon oncle. **5** au onzième étage **6** aux États-Unis **7** à Londres **8** Le professeur a pris le cahier à l'élève.

Pour (p38)

1 This *is* the train going to Lyon? **2** a paper plane **3** I spoke to my teacher for twenty minutes. **4** I'm going to Canada for three weeks. **5** He is intelligent enough to pass his examination. **6** He is too ill to travel.

Prepositions of position (p39)

1 en face de la Poste **2** au-dessus de la ville **3** sur la table **4** contre le mur **5** entre la forêt et le lac **6** devant le supermarché **7** à droite de la salle à manger **8** à gauche du cinéma **9** à côté de la boulangerie **10** dans la valise **11** loin de la ville **12** près de la gare **13** derrière la maison **14** sous la chaise **15** à côté de la piscine et du camping.

Prepositions linking verbs to their objects (p39)

1 Nous avons cherché le voleur.   **2** Il habitait Madrid.   **3** J'ai attendu un autobus.   **4** L'agent a pris le revolver au voleur.   **5** Elle a montré les bananes à la dame.   **6** Il écoutait la musique.   **7** L'agent a regardé la voiture.   **8** Elle a donné la réponse au professeur.   **9** Il a vendu son vélo à son ami.   **10** Ils ont téléphoné à la police.

Pronouns (p40)

1 I asked them the reason.   **2** The gentleman sold him the car.
3 He saw me at the Post Office.   **4** I'll write to you next week.   **5** I'm going to speak to you later in the day.   **6** Your books? I saw them in the hall.   **7** You'll write to me, won't you?   **8** They had been allowed to go out.   **9** I told her to come home early, but she hasn't come back yet.   **10** He asked me to put my pipe out.   **11** Je ne les comprends pas.
12 Je lui ai téléphoné la semaine dernière.   **13** Je lui parlerai demain.
14 Le film? Je l'ai vu à la télé hier soir.   **15** Il a demandé l'heure à Alain.   **16** Il nous parle.   **17** Je voudrais les voir dans mon bureau.
18 Je lui ai parlé mardi dernier.   **19** Tu m'entends?   **20** Il lui a montré son permis de conduire.

Y, en, on (p41)

1 He had seen his father there.   **2** Have you got a biro? I've got two.
3 She hasn't got any cousins. Oh yes she has! She's got one.   **4** She's going there next Tuesday.   **5** We shall see.   **6** We shall be back home around five o'clock.   **7** People drink more wine in France than in England.   **8** I was woken at four a.m.   **9** We enjoyed ourselves, didn't we?   **10** He was told to keep quiet.

Useful constructions for your essay (p43)

1 J'étais en train de laver la voiture quand il est arrivé.   **2** Nous venions d'arriver.   **3** Vous parlez depuis une demi-heure.   **4** Elle était sur le point d'entrer dans la maison.   **5** Avant de finir le travail il a fumé une cigarette.   **6** Il travaillait sans parler.   **7** Nous travaillons pour gagner de l'argent.   **8** Je viens d'arriver.   **9** Il attendait depuis longtemps.   **10** Après être monté au dixième étage j'étais fatigué.
11 Après avoir fini son travail elle s'est reposée.   **12** Après s'être peignée, elle s'est habillée.

Revising vocabulary

1 L'identité (p47)

A 1 Elle a dix-huit ans. **2** Je suis né le 2 janvier 1965. **3** Il avait les yeux verts et les cheveux noirs. **4** Elle est fille unique. **5** Mon frère est professeur. **6** Ma sœur est élève d'un CES. **7** Je suis élève de cette école depuis six ans. **8** Je suis un mordu du sport.

B My father was born in 1937, two years before the Second World War. After the war he became an engineer and he's been doing this job for more than thirty years now. My mother used to work part-time until recently, but now she's a housewife. It's a job without pay which however demands a lot of effort. And me? I was born in 1964 in a small town in the west of France. As I was fortunate to be born in a period of women's liberation, I am quite determined to take full advantage of these equalities of opportunity.

C 1(c) 2(b) 3(a)

2 La maison, l'appartement (p49)

A We are lucky to live in a house – unlike the majority of French people who are obliged to live in large blocks of flats. Our house is a bit old fashioned, but all the same you feel at home. The rooms are of a decent size, with a large living-room on the ground floor. Our family is large and as I'm the youngest I've been given a little room in the attic; it only measures 3 metres by 2. Despite its size, I like it very much, with its light green wallpaper. The atmosphere of this old house has brought us a lot of joy over the years, which proves that twentieth-century gadgets – micro-wave ovens, warm-air heating, dishwashers – which everybody seems to be obsessed with, are not as essential as the advertisements would have us believe.

B 1(c) 2(c) 3(c) 4(a)

3 La routine quotidienne (p51)

A 1 M. Snobinard s'est réveillé quinze minutes avant sa femme. **2** Elle s'est levée tout de suite et s'est lavée. **3** Je me suis habillé et me suis peigné. **4** Ils sont descendus pour prendre leur petit déjeuner. **5** Elle prenait du café noir et mangeait du pain quand l'homme est arrivé. **6** Ils sont entrés dans la salle en se dépêchant. **7** Je me brossais les dents avant de me coucher. **8** Ils se sont mis en route pour l'église. **9** Je faisais le ménage et mon mari faisait la vaisselle. **10** Ils sont sortis en vélo. **11** J'ai fait une promenade mardi après-midi. **12** Les enfants se sont couchés tard. **13** Elle a renversé le café. **14** Il a laissé tomber le disque.

B 1 se peigner **2** se brosser les dents **3** s'habiller **4** se raser **5** se dépêcher **6** faire la vaisselle **7** faire le ménage **8** faire une promenade.

C 1(b) 2(a) 3(c)

4 La nourriture (p53)

A 1 Il prenait le petit déjeuner dans la cuisine.   **2** Il buvait un verre
de vin rouge quand la jeune fille est entrée dans le restaurant.   **3** Comme
hors d'œuvre il a choisi un œuf mayonnaise.   **4** Ils ont pris un repas
léger – du poisson garni de légumes.   **5** Il a commandé un café noir.
6 Le garçon a apporté le dessert.   **7** Elle recevait des invités pour le
dîner.

B 1(d) 2(a) 3(b) 4(b)

5 Les passe-temps (p55)

A Everyone fills up his free time in a way which is enjoyable to him, but
sometimes you find people with strange tastes. My brother-in-law, for
example, is never happier than when he is doing do-it-yourself jobs,
despite his lack of skill. My sister told me about an incident when her
husband tried to mend a leak in a radiator. The slight leak became a
serious one and they ended up sending for the plumber! But when it
comes down to it, this lack of skill doesn't matter. What is more important
is the pleasure and relaxation after a long day of work.

B 1(a) 2(a) 3(b) 4(c)

6 Cinéma, théâtre, télévision, radio (p57)

A 1 Il avait pris trois places au balcon.   **2** Ils ont dû faire la queue pour
prendre des billets au guichet.   **3** L'homme a décidé d'offrir un
pourboire à l'ouvreuse.   **4** Il lui a montré son billet et elle l'a conduit à
sa place.   **5** Il dormait devant le téléviseur quand l'émission a
commencé.   **6** La séance s'est terminée à minuit.

B 1(c) 2(c) 3(c)
C 1(a) 2(c) 3(a)

7 Les sports (p59)

A 1 Il jouait au tennis quand ses parents sont arrivés.   **2** L'équipe de
Strasbourg a battu l'équipe de Metz.   **3** Ils perdraient le match mais
gagneraient quand même un prix.   **4** Ils encourageaient leur fille aux
matches de hockey.   **5** Nous allons regarder le match à la télé.

B 1(c) 2(a) 3(d) 4(a)

8 La ville (p61)

A 1 Notre maison est située dans un quartier résidentiel.   **2** Nous
habitons à cinq kilomètres du centre de la ville.   **3** Tous les samedis
plusieurs centaines de touristes font une visite guidée de la cathédrale.
4 Il y avait beaucoup de monde sur le trottoir.

B 1(a) 2(c) 3(a)

9 Les magasins (1) (p63)

A Mrs Orteil was about to complete her shopping list – she had almost forgotten the bottle of suntan lotion for going away on holiday. When she had finished off her list she set off for the high street. The butcher greeted her when she went into his shop – she was a regular customer:
– Good morning, madam. Can I help you?
– A nice piece of beef – about one kilo – but not too fatty please.
– Is that OK for you?
– Perfect.
– Anything else, madam?
– That's all, thanks.
    Then she went on to the grocer's.
– I'd like half a kilo of Brussels sprouts, please.
– I'm terribly sorry, madam, I'm out of Brussels sprouts.
– Well I'll take two cauliflowers. How much are they each?
– Two francs ten, madam.

As she wanted to buy a wedding present for a friend she went into a store. She was really spoilt for choice. In the household products department she saw an electric coffee-maker – but with a price tag of 160 francs! She ought to have found something less expensive, but her friend would appreciate this nice present. She made her purchase and explained to the saleswoman that she was going to give it as a present. The saleswoman wrapped up the coffee-maker in special paper.

10 Les magasins (2) (p65)

A 1 La vendeuse se tenait derrière le comptoir.   2 La cliente est entrée dans le magasin.   3 Il y avait beaucoup de monde à la caisse.
4 Le marché avait lieu le lundi et le vendredi.   5 Elle a examiné les pommes et a decidé d'en acheter un kilo.   6 Elle a mis les deux kilos d'oranges et le kilo de bananes dans son panier.   7 Elle a dit au revoir au marchand et a quitté le magasin.   8 Le marchand a servi le client.
B 1 un marché   2 le vendeur   3 la cliente   4 un comptoir   5 la caisse.

    C 1(c) 2(c) 3(a)

11 L'école (p67)
    A 1(a) 2(a) 3(b) 4(c)

12 Au-delà de l'école (p69)

A 1 Il est devenu médecin.   2 Il trouvera un emploi dans une usine.
3 Elle s'intéressait à devenir institutrice.   4 Ma mère est employée de bureau.   5 Quand je quitterai l'école je veux être ingénieur.
    B 1(c) 2(a) 3(b) 4(c)

13 Les transports (p71)

A 1 Ils ont fait la queue pour passer la douane.   2 Il a pris un billet au conducteur.   3 Il a pris un autobus de l'aéroport au centre-ville. 4 J'ai fait le voyage en car.   5 Elle est montée dans l'autobus.   6 M. et Mme Delage ont dû descendre du train tout de suite.

  B 1(b) 2(a) 3(b)

14 Les chemins de fer (p73)

A 1 L'homme a pris un aller et retour, deuxième classe, pour Lyon au guichet.   2 Le train est parti de la gare à l'heure.   3 Je n'aime pas voyager la nuit.   4 Parce qu'il avait soif il est passé au buffet.   5 Le voyageur s'est renseigné sur l'horaire des trains.   6 Il avait loué une voiture.   7 Les deux jeunes filles sont montées dans la voiture.   8 Les trois garçons sont descendus du train à Calais.   9 Le train est arrivé en retard.   10 Le porteur portait deux valises.

  B 1(c) 2(c) 3(a) 4(a) 5(b)

15 La voiture (1) (p75)

A 1 Il vérifiait toujours les pneus, l'huile, l'eau et l'essence.   2 Ils se sont arrêtés à une station de service.   3 J'aime rouler sur les routes nationales.   4 Le chauffeur de taxi a ouvert le coffre.   5 Ils ont garé la voiture dans un parking.   6 Elle a conduit pendant deux heures, puis est descendue de la voiture.   7 L'automobiliste est monté dans sa voiture.   8 Il a acheté vingt litres de super.

  B 1(c) 2(a) 3(c) 4(c) 5(b)

16 La voiture (2) (p77)

A Le camion a brûlé le feu rouge et est rentré dans une grande voiture noire. Heureusement personne n'a été gravement blessé et l'automobiliste a pu téléphoner à la police. Une voiture de police est arrivée bientôt et l'agent a demandé aux conducteurs de montrer leurs permis. Le conducteur du camion a dû accompagner l'agent au commissariat le plus proche. Plus tard il a attrapé une amende.

  C 1(c) 2(a)

17 Les fêtes (p79)

A 1 Il avait congé le lundi matin et travaillait le samedi après-midi. 2 Ils sont partis le lendemain.   3 Je ne travaille pas le dimanche. 4 Ils ont décidé de fêter son anniversaire.   5 Les vacances de Noël durent une quinzaine.   6 Les grandes vacances avaient commencé la veille.   7 Il est arrivé jeudi dernier.   8 Mes vacances se termineront le 21 août.   9 'Joyeux Noël,' a dit Paul.   10 'Bonne année!' a-t-il répondu.   11 Il a consulté son agenda.   12 Ils consultaient le calendrier quand elle est arrivée.

  B 1(b) 2(c) 3(a) 4(c) 5(a)

18 Les vacances (p81)

A 1 Ils ont décidé de faire un séjour en France. **2** Nous allons passer trois semaines à la montagne. **3** J'ai fait un échange avec une jeune fille française. **4** J'ai passé deux semaines agréables à une auberge de jeunesse. **5** Elle est entrée dans une agence de voyages. **6** C'était une région intéressante.

B 1(b) 2(a) 3(d)

19 Au bord de la mer (p83)

A 1 Nous allons passer quinze jours sur la côte sud de l'Angleterre. **2** Ils avaient passé l'après-midi à faire de la pêche.   Je n'attrapais jamais rien. **4** Je viens de prendre un bain de soleil sur la plage. **5** Elle mettait son maillot de bain quand il a commencé à pleuvoir. **6** Ils ont acheté une glace au marchand de glaces. **7** L'homme a crié au secours. Il se noyait. **8** Il ne savait pas nager. **9** On a pu le sauver. **10** Je m'ennuyais. **11** Nous nous sommes bien amusés pendant les quinze jours au bord de la mer.

B 1(b) 2(a) 3(a)

20 La campagne (p85)

A 1 La famille a fait une sortie à la campagne. **2** Ils ont décidé de manger sur l'herbe au bord de la route. **3** J'adore les forêts et les lacs. **4** La guêpe venait de le piquer. **5** Ils bavardaient avec quelques paysans. **6** Le fermier s'est fâché parce qu'ils avaient laissé la barrière ouverte. **7** Le taureau a poursuivi les deux jeunes garçons. **8** Un chemin traversait le pré.

B 1(c) 2(c) 3(c) 4(c)

21 L'hôtel (p87)

A 1 Ils sont descendus à un hôtel ce soir-là. **2** Nous avons pris une chambre à deux lits. **3** Il a pris une douche dans sa salle de bain privée. **4** Nous nous sommes renseignés au syndicat d'initiative. **5** Elle est descendue dans l'ascenseur. **6** M. Lorne a réglé la facture et est parti. **7** Le propriétaire a dit que nous n'avions pas réservé la chambre à l'avance. **8** Cet hôtel-là était complet; nous devions trouver un autre ce soir-là. **9** Nous avons offert un pourboire à la femme de chambre.

B 1(a) 2(a) 3(b)

22 Le temps (p89)

A 1 Le jour de leur départ en vacances il faisait du brouillard. **2** Il gèle en décembre. **3** L'été dernier il a fait beau. **4** Quand nous sommes arrivés il faisait du vent et il pleuvait. **5** Vous avez besoin de porter un parapluie quand il fait mauvais.

B 1 gèle **2** printemps **3** temps **4** brouillard

C 1(b) 2(a) 3(c) 4(b)

23 L'heure (p91)

B 1 Elle est arrivée tôt. 2 M. Grossetête était arrivé en retard à son bureau. 3 Ils ont passé deux heures à écouter la radio. 4 Elle a passé toute la journée à écrire des lettres. 5 Il était huit heures précises à la pendule du salon. 6 Sa montre avançait de vingt minutes. 7 Il a consulté sa montre : il était à l'heure. 8 L'horloge de l'église a sonné onze heures comme il quittait le supermarché. 9 Le réveil a sonné à six heures vingt du matin. 10 Ils ont passé une matinée intéressante. 11 La soirée était très fatigante. 12 J'ai fini le travail il y a un quart d'heure.

  B 1 une montre 2 une horloge 3 un réveil 4 une pendule
  C 1(c) 2(a) 3(c)

24 La santé (p93)

B 1 Il s'était blessé le bras. 2 Il s'est coupé le doigt. 3 J'ai mal aux oreilles. 4 Elle avait mal à la tête. 5 Je viens d'attraper un rhume et j'ai de la fièvre. 6 Il s'est rétabli trois jours plus tard. 7 Il avait mal au cœur après le repas. 8 Ma mère est tombée malade. 9 Ils ont été gravement blessés dans l'accident. 10 Ses blessures étaient graves.

  B 1(b) 2(a) 3(a)

25 Le corps (p95)

B At present thousands of people are beginning to realize that physical exercise not only keeps you fit, but can also enrich your way of life. The physical benefits are not to be denied and concern a whole series of organs and muscles in the body – lungs, heart, legs, knees, back, arms – but people who are very keen on jogging, for example, also talk about an inner calm which is highly therapeutic, especially for the businessman suffering from stress. Diet also plays its part, which is just as important as that of exercise. In order to keep in trim, you are not obliged to follow an exotic diet but rather to reduce your intake of sweet things. It is very much in your interest to develop such habits and attitudes in your youth, if you want to live to a ripe old age. A nice figure and a life-style which is still active are not out of the question even when you are turned sixty.

  B 1(a) 2(b) 3(c) 4(a)

26 Les vêtements (p97)

A 1 Il portait une veste verte et un pantalon bleu. 2 Elle a essayé le tricot mais il ne lui allait pas bien. 3 Elle portait une jupe blanche.

  B 1 un chapeau 2 un imper 3 la chemisette 4 des gants 5 un tricot.

  C 1(c) 2(b) 3(c) 4(b)

27 Les animaux (p99)

A 1 Il promenait le chien quand l'accident est arrivé. 2 Elle avait peur des souris. 3 Le chien est sorti dans la rue en courant. 4 Les lions se sont évadés de leur cage. 5 Les chasseurs ont dû tirer sur la bête féroce. 6 L'ours venait de s'évader du cirque.

B The children, when they noticed the bear, stood still. The idea of running away did not even occur to them. The bear had moved forward, watching them. His eyes were glinting. Then he turned his head away. Jérôme had just moved forward. Perhaps he was so frightened that he no longer knew what he was doing. He stopped a few steps away from the bear which was standing on its hind legs.

C 1(c) 2(b) 3(a) 4(b)

28 Quelques pays (p101)

A 1 l'Espagne 2 la Grande-Bretagne 3 la Suisse 4 la Belgique 5 le Japon 6 le Canada 7 la Russie 8 les États-Unis.

B 1(c) 2(a) 3(a)

29 Le crime ne paie pas (p103)

A 1 Ils ont entendu un bruit qui venait d'en bas. 2 Les voleurs se sont sauvés. 3 On a emmené les cambrioleurs au commissariat. 4 J'ai téléphoné à la police. 5 Ils avaient volé une voiture.

B One day I was sitting at a café terrace, taking advantage of a few minutes' break to glance at my newspaper. On the front page there was an article on a break-in at a local chemist's. A large quantity of drugs had disappeared. The details of the theft were followed by a description of the two men the police were looking for. I had just put my paper on the table and was about to have my coffee when I noticed a sinister character at the next table. I picked up my paper again and re-read the description: he really was one of the criminals, I was convinced. When I had settled my bill, I went into the café to find a telephone box. A police car arrived at high speed and three policemen got out, revolvers in their hands. The criminal gave himself up with the minimum of resistance, without trying to escape. The police were very pleased to have arrested this criminal. Within a few days they had found the accomplice and recovered the stolen drugs. And me? I received a reward from the chemist for having recognized this sinister character from the description in the newspaper.

C 1 poursuivre 2 tenait 3 reconnu 4 évader 5 voisins 6 en bas.

Getting ready for the examination

Translation from French (pp110–11)

A Tenses 1 He would like to work in Turkey. **2** I'm not working at the moment. **3** I've just seen them. **4** He was going to school when the accident happened. **5** After he had entered the room he said hullo to me. **6** I had been waiting for ten minutes. **7** She had got up. **8** Do you drink a litre of wine per day? **9** He came at seven o'clock. **10** I have been a pupil of this school for six years. **11** When I was younger I used to go to the cinema on Saturday mornings, but that doesn't interest me any longer. **12** I've been smoking for two years. **13** He was amazed. **14** You had just arrived, hadn't you? **15** What will your father do when he retires?

B Verb ending -ant 1 He hurried down. **2** He ran in. **3** He hurried off. **4** He ran out.

C Reflexives 1 This work is easily done. **2** The door closed. **3** I shaved at eight o'clock. **4** 'Where is he?' the policeman wondered. **5** I washed my face.

D On 1 Shall we pay? **2** The work was started at six o'clock. **3** I was told that . . . **4** They were asked whether . . . **5** The battle was won.

E Infinitives 1 He decided to leave. **2** We ended up by saying goodbye to him. **3** You've succeeded in convincing us. **4** I can hear someone whistling in this classroom. **5** Watching telly every evening? That wouldn't interest me in the least.

F Word order 1 A friend whose sister-in-law I know. **2** An author whose novels I read frequently. **3** The impression my pupils made was pathetic.

G Articles 1 I hate cheese. **2** I find it difficult to believe you. **3** Virtue has its rewards. **4** The man with the white beard. **5** I cut my finger.

H Word for word translations 1 I was thirsty because it was hot. **2** One swallow doesn't make a summer. **3** I feel I'm in top condition – I'm as fit as a fiddle! **4** She's in a very bad mood – she must have got out of bed on the wrong side this morning.

I Vocabulary 1 However **2** none the less **3** repeatedly **4** rather
5 occasionally **6** from time to time **7** however **8** formerly
9 several **10** later **11** on time **12** in the end **13** previously
14 according to **15** despite **16** soon **17** too **18** enough **19** once
20 at the present time.

Prose composition (pp118–19)

1 Ce soir-là John s'est couché tard. Quand il a ouvert les yeux il a vu
qu'il était déjà huit heures et demie. Il devait être à l'usine à neuf
heures. Il s'est levé, s'est habillé et a décidé de ne pas se raser. Il a bu
une tasse de café et est sorti dans la rue en se précipitant.

Il n'y avait personne là. Même le marchand de journaux qui était
d'habitude au coin était déjà parti. John a commencé à attendre
l'autobus. Un quart d'heure plus tard il était toujours là, et il n'avait
vu que quelques enfants. En fin de compte il a vu un taxi qui s'est
arrêté presque aussitôt.

John y est monté et le taxi a démarré. 'Roulez aussi vite que
possible,' a dit John au chauffeur. 'Heureusement il n'y a pas beaucoup
de circulation.' L'homme avait l'air étonné. Quand ils sont arrivés à
l'usine, John a vu que les portes étaient fermées. Puis il s'est rappelé
que c'était dimanche. Il est rentré à pied.

2 Il y a quatre ans environ, je marchais le long du trottoir quand j'ai
remarqué soudain un vieil ami assis devant un café de l'autre côté de
la rue.

Comme je ne l'avais pas vu récemment, j'ai traversé la rue pour lui
parler. 'Salut, comment ça va?' lui ai-je demandé. 'Qu'est-ce que tu
fais là? Est-ce que tu attends quelqu'un?'

'Non, personne,' a-t-il répondu, en me serrant la main. 'Je suis
arrivé en ville hier soir. Je viens de terminer mes études et je prends
quelques jours de congé avant de chercher un emploi.'

Après avoir bavardé longtemps nous avons décidé de déjeuner
ensemble dans un restaurant à côté que nous connaissions assez bien.
Pendant le repas, il m'a invité à aller le voir ce soir-là.

3 Il faisait nuit quand ils sont entrés dans le château fort. Ils ont monté
deux étages et sont venus à un long couloir où il y avait beaucoup de
pièces. 'A droite,' a chuchoté Victor – 'la quatrième pièce au fond.'
Ils ont bientôt trouvé la porte mais elle était fermée à clef. Après
environ dix minutes ils ont pu l'ouvrir, et y sont entrés. Beauchamp a
vu le lit où son père dormait. Il l'a réveillé doucement. 'C'est moi,
Philippe, et un ami. N'aie pas peur. Lève-toi, mais ne dis pas un mot.'
Le père s'est habillé, mais comme ils étaient sur le point de quitter la
pièce, il a dit d'une voix basse: 'Je ne suis pas le seul prisonnier ici. Il
y a aussi une jeune fille, mais je ne la connais pas.' 'C'est
probablement Mademoiselle Boudard,' a dit Victor. 'Je ne la connais

pas, mais je l'ai vue plusieurs fois dans le parc.' 'Est-ce que tu sais où se trouve sa chambre?' 'Oui, je crois qu'elle est en face de la mienne.' 'C'est la pièce bleue,' a murmuré Victor. 'Il ne sera pas trop difficile d'ouvrir cette porte-là.'

Le père de Beauchamp est entré dans la pièce et cinq minutes plus tard il est sorti avec la jeune fille et a dit à Victor et à son fils: 'Vous avez raison; c'est bien Mademoiselle Boudard.' Ils sont tous descendus doucement et sont sortis sur la terrasse où leurs amis attendaient.

4 Susan Thorpe attendait Colette, sa correspondante française, à l'aéroport de Londres. Il était dix heures vingt et l'avion de Colette venait d'arriver, avec un peu de retard. Bientôt Susan a vu une jeune fille aux cheveux blonds qui avait l'air très élégant. Elle a souri. 'C'est Susan, n'est-ce pas?' Susan, qui portait un pantalon et une vieille chemise, a rougi et a répondu: 'Oui, je suis Susan. J'espère que tu seras heureuse chez nous. Viens avec moi; papa est là-bas dans la voiture.'

Pendant le voyage Colette a posé à son amie beaucoup de questions. Elle voulait savoir si Susan allait au théâtre, si elle sortait beaucoup le soir, si elle fumait, et si elle s'intéressait à l'histoire. La pauvre Susan, qui adorait le sport et n'aimait pas la lecture, a décidé que cette visite n'était pas une très bonne idée après tout. Cependant, elle avait tort, les deux jeunes filles ont passé un mois très agréable ensemble et puis elles sont allées en France.

Reading comprehension (pp123–4)

(a) 1 Il avait espéré qu'on lui rendrait son fils.   2 Il ne le rendait pas parce qu'il avait quelques problèmes.   3 On le sait parce que le 'kidnapper' a dit qu'il rappellerait le narrateur.   4 Il se rendait à l'école quand on l'a enlevé.   5 Il avait huit ans à ce moment-là.   6 Il menaçait de tuer le petit garçon.   7 Sa femme l'a prévenu après le coup de téléphone du 'kidnapper'.
(b) 8 Il a regardé par la fenêtre après avoir allumé une cigarette.
9 Elle s'est assise dans un fauteuil sans rien dire.   10 Elle n'avait pas fermé la porte à clef.   11 Il était en train de lire des documents.   12 Elle les a passées à parcourir des yeux une vieille bibliothèque remplie de livres.   13 Elle est venue persuader Georges de lui donnner un peu d'argent.   14 Il lui a dit de le laisser tranquille.

Listening comprehension (pp132–3)

1 The sunlight coming into the author's bedroom at five a.m. woke him up. **2** Village primary school teacher. **3** It had a white ceiling, whitewood furniture, with a fairly bright atmosphere. **4** There was a river flowing through some green fields in a valley. **5** He suddenly thought of the fish in the river and wanted to go fishing. **6** He had forbidden him to go to the river alone, feeling responsible for his safety in the absence of the parents and worried because of newspaper reports of children drowning. **7** He opened his door quietly and went through his uncle's bedroom on tiptoe. **8** He was frightened that the noise of his boots would waken his uncle. **9** He heard the church bell and trembled. **10** He had a calm expression which looked even gentler as he slept. **11** He was tempted to shout to him to get up and to suggest they go to the river together, so that his uncle would benefit from the morning air and have a good appetite when they came back. **12** He went down the stairs and went out into the garden.

Listening comprehension (pp135–7)

1(d) (2a) 3(b) 4(e) 5(c) 6(d) 7(c) 8(e) 9(e) 10(a) 11(b) 12(c)

Oral pictures

A 1 Non, il vient d'y arriver. **2** Ils monteront dans le train.
3 L'employé a laissé tomber un de ses sacs. **B 1** Elle doit payer deux cent quarante-huit francs vingt-cinq. **2** Elle lui rendra cinquante francs de monnaie. **3** Il y a beaucoup de rayons, avec un grand choix de produits. **C 1** Non, elles viennent de tomber. **2** Il a neigé.
3 Elle les offrira à sa maman, peut-être. **4** Non, il est toujours en train de travailler. **D 1** Sa sœur a cassé une assiette. **2** Elle est en train de donner à boire au chat. **3** Il a été méchant, peut-être. **E 1** Non, ils sont toujours en train de manger. **2** Elle choisira un dessert. **3** Il veut ramasser sa serviette et son couteau qu'il a laissés tomber. **F 1** Il nettoyait les vitrines d'un grand magasin. **2** Elle s'arrêtera, peut-être! **3** Non, il y est allé pour faire des achats et pour promener son chien.

Verb tables

REGULAR VERBS

-ER type   travailler (to work)

Present Tense

je travaille	nous travaillons
tu travailles	vous travaillez
il travaille	ils travaillent

Future

je travaillerai	nous travaillerons
tu travailleras	vous travaillerez
il travaillera	ils travailleront

Imperfect

je travaillais	nous travaillions
tu travaillais	vous travailliez
il travaillait	ils travaillaient

Conditional

je travaillerais	nous travaillerions
tu travaillerais	vous travailleriez
il travaillerait	ils travailleraient

Perfect

j'ai travaillé	nous avons travaillé
tu as travaillé	vous avez travaillé
il a travaillé	ils ont travaillé

Commands

travaille!
travaillons!
travaillez!

Past Historic

il travailla	nous
ils travaillèrent	

-IR type   finir (to finish)

Present Tense

je finis	nous finissons
tu finis	vous finissez
il finit	ils finissent

Future

je finirai	nous finirons
tu finiras	vous finirez
il finira	ils finiront

Imperfect

je finissais	nous finissions
tu finissais	vous finissiez
il finissait	ils finissaient

Conditional

je finirais	nous finirions
tu finirais	vous finiriez
il finirait	ils finiraient

Perfect

j'ai fini	nous avons fini
tu as fini	vous avez fini
il a fini	ils ont fini

Commands

finis!
finissons!
finissez!

Past Historic

il finit	
ils finirent	

REGULAR VERBS—continued

-RE type vendre (to sell)

Present Tense
je vends   nous vendons
tu vends   vous vendez
il vend   ils vendent

Future
je vendrai   nous vendrons
tu vendras   vous vendrez
il vendra   ils vendront

Imperfect
je vendais   nous vendions
tu vendais   vous vendiez
il vendait   ils vendaient

Conditional
je vendrais   nous vendrions
tu vendrais   vous vendriez
il vendrait   ils vendraient

Perfect
j'ai vendu   nous avons vendu
tu as vendu   vous avez vendu
il a vendu   ils ont vendu

Past Historic
il vendit   ils vendirent

Commands
vends!
vendons!
vendez!

REGULAR REFLEXIVE VERBS.

Endings as above according to whether -er, -ir or -re type. An -er type is given in full as an example

se dépêcher (to hurry)

Present
je me dépêche   nous nous dépêchons
tu te dépêches   vous vous dépêchez
il se dépêche   ils se dépêchent

Future
je me dépêcherai   nous nous dépêcherons
tu te dépêcheras   vous vous dépêcherez
il se dépêchera   ils se dépêcheront

Imperfect
je me dépêchais   nous nous dépêchions
tu te dépêchais   vous vous dépêchiez
il se dépêchait   ils se dépêchaient

Conditional
je me dépêcherais   nous nous dépêcherions
tu te dépêcherais   vous vous dépêcheriez
il se dépêcherait   ils se dépêcheraient

Perfect
je me suis dépêché   nous nous sommes dépêchés
tu t'es dépêché   vous vous êtes dépêchés
il s'est dépêché   ils se sont dépêchés

Past Historic
il se dépêcha   ils se dépêchèrent

Commands
dépêche-toi!
dépêchons-nous!
dépêchez-vous!

IRREGULAR VERBS. Where a tense is not given in full, assume the *endings* follow the same pattern as the ones given for regular -er, -ir and -re types. The column marked perfect reminds you whether the verb takes avoir or être in that tense and gives the past participle.

Infinitive	Present Tense	Imperfect	Perfect	Future	Conditional	Command	Past Historic
être (to be)	je suis tu es il est nous sommes vous êtes ils sont	j'étais tu étais il était nous étions vous étiez ils étaient	j'ai été tu as été etc.	je serai tu seras etc.	je serais tu serais etc.	sois! soyons! soyez!	il fut ils furent
avoir (to have)	j'ai tu as il a nous avons vous avez ils ont	j'avais tu avais il avait nous avions vous aviez ils avaient	j'ai eu tu as eu etc.	j'aurai tu auras etc.	j'aurais tu aurais etc.	aie! ayons! ayez!	il eut ils eurent
faire (to do, to make)	je fais tu fais il fait nous faisons vous faites ils font	je faisais tu faisais etc.	j'ai fait tu as fait etc.	je ferai tu feras etc.	je ferais tu ferais etc.	fais! faisons! faites!	il fit ils firent
aller (to go)	je vais tu vas il va nous allons vous allez ils vont	j'allais tu allais etc.	je suis allé tu es allé etc.	j'irai tu iras etc.	j'irais tu irais etc.	va! allons! allez!	il alla ils allèrent
devoir (to have to, to be obliged to, 'must')	je dois tu dois il doit nous devons vous devez ils doivent	je devais tu devais etc.	j'ai dû tu as dû etc.	je devrai tu devras etc.	je devrais tu devrais etc.	— — —	il dut ils durent
pouvoir (to be able, 'can')	je peux tu peux il peut nous pouvons vous pouvez ils peuvent	je pouvais tu pouvais etc.	j'ai pu tu as pu etc.	je pourrai tu pourras etc.	je pourrais tu pourrais etc.	— — —	il put ils purent
savoir (to know) [how to]	je sais tu sais il sait nous savons vous savez ils savent	je savais tu savais etc.	j'ai su tu as su etc.	je saurai tu sauras etc.	je saurais tu saurais etc.	— — —	il sut ils surent
conduire (to drive)	je conduis tu conduis il conduit nous conduisons vous conduisez ils conduisent	je conduisais tu conduisais etc.	j'ai conduit tu as conduit etc.	je conduirai tu conduiras etc.	je conduirais tu conduirais etc.	conduis! conduisons! conduisez!	il conduisit ils conduisirent
détruire (to destroy)	je détruis tu détruis il détruit nous détruisons vous détruisez ils détruisent	je détruisais tu détruisais etc.	j'ai détruit tu as détruit etc.	je détruirai tu détruiras etc.	je détruirais tu détruirais etc.	détruis! détruisons! détruisez!	il détruisit ils détruisirent
construire (to construct)	exactly the same pattern as détruire but with cons- instead of dé- as the first letters je construis, tu construis etc.						
connaître (to know, to be familiar with)	je connais tu connais il connaît nous connaissons vous connaissez ils connaissent	je connaissais tu connaissais etc.	j'ai connu tu as connu etc.	je connaîtrai tu connaîtras etc.	je connaîtrais tu connaîtrais etc.	— —	il connut ils connurent

IRREGULAR VERBS—continued

Infinitive	Present tense	Imperfect	Perfect	Future	Conditional	Command	Past Historic
reconnaître (to recognize)	exactly the same pattern as connaître but with re- as the first two letters je reconnais, tu reconnais etc.						
paraître (to appear)	exactly the same pattern as connaître but with par- replacing conn- as the first letters je parais, tu parais etc.						
disparaître (to disappear)	exactly the same pattern as connaître but with dispar- replacing conn- as the first letters je disparais, tu disparais etc.						
ouvrir (to open)	j'ouvre, tu ouvres, il ouvre, nous ouvrons, vous ouvrez, ils ouvrent	j'ouvrais, tu ouvrais etc.	j'ai ouvert, tu as ouvert etc.	j'ouvrirai, tu ouvriras etc.	j'ouvrirais, tu ouvrirais etc.	ouvre! ouvrons! ouvrez!	il ouvrit, ils ouvrirent
couvrir (to cover)	exactly the same pattern as ouvrir but with c as the first letter je couvre, tu couvres etc.						
souffrir (to suffer)	je souffre, tu souffres, il souffre, nous souffrons, vous souffrez, ils souffrent	je souffrais, tu souffrais etc.	j'ai souffert, tu as souffert etc.	je souffrirai, tu souffriras etc.	je souffrirais, tu souffrirais etc.	— —	il souffrit, ils souffrirent
mettre (to put)	je mets, tu mets, il met, nous mettons, vous mettez, ils mettent	je mettais, tu mettais etc.	j'ai mis, tu as mis etc.	je mettrai, tu mettras etc.	je mettrais, tu mettrais etc.	mets! mettons! mettez!	il mit, ils mirent
promettre (to promise)	exactly the same pattern as mettre with pro- as the first three letters						
prendre (to take)	je prends, tu prends, il prend, nous prenons, vous prenez, ils prennent	je prenais, tu prenais etc.	j'ai pris, tu as pris etc.	je prendrai, tu prendras etc.	je prendrais, tu prendrais etc.	prends! prenons! prenez!	il prit, ils prirent
comprendre (to understand)	exactly the same pattern as prendre with com- as the first three letters						
apprendre (to learn)	exactly the same pattern as prendre with ap- as the first two letters j'apprends, tu apprends etc.						
sortir (to go out)	je sors, tu sors, il sort, nous sortons, vous sortez, ils sortent	je sortais, tu sortais etc.	je suis sorti, tu es sorti etc.	je sortirai, tu sortiras etc.	je sortirais, tu sortirais etc.	sors! sortons! sortez!	il sortit, ils sortirent
partir (to depart)	je pars, tu pars, il part, nous partons, vous partez, ils partent	je partais, tu partais etc.	je suis parti, tu es parti etc.	je partirai, tu partiras etc.	je partirais, tu partirais etc.	pars! partons! partez!	il partit, ils partirent
dormir (to sleep)	je dors, tu dors, il dort, nous dormons, vous dormez, ils dorment	je dormais, tu dormais etc.	j'ai dormi, tu as dormi etc.	je dormirai, tu dormiras etc.	je dormirais, tu dormirais etc.	dors! dormons! dormez!	il dormit, ils dormirent

IRREGULAR *VERBS—continued*

Infinitive	Present Tense	Imperfect	Perfect	Future	Conditional	Command	Past Historic
servir (to serve)	je sers tu sers il sert	je servais tu servais etc.	j'ai servi tu as servi etc.	je servirai tu serviras etc.	je servirais tu servirais etc.	sers! servons! servez!	il servit ils servirent
recevoir (to receive)	je reçois tu reçois il reçoit nous recevons vous recevez ils reçoivent	je recevais tu recevais etc.	j'ai reçu tu as reçu etc.	je recevrai tu recevras etc.	je recevrais tu recevrais etc.	reçois! recevons! recevez!	il reçut ils reçurent
vouloir (to want, wish)	je veux tu veux il veut nous voulons vous voulez ils veulent	je voulais tu voulais etc.	j'ai voulu tu as voulu etc.	je voudrai tu voudras etc.	je voudrais tu voudrais etc.	— — —	il voulut ils voulurent
venir (to come)	je viens tu viens il vient nous venons vous venez ils viennent	je venais tu venais etc.	je suis venu tu es venu etc.	je viendrai tu viendras etc.	je viendrais tu viendrais etc.	viens! venons! venez!	il vint ils vinrent
devenir (to become)	exactly the same pattern as venir with de- as the first two letters						
prévenir (to inform, to warn)	exactly the same pattern as venir with pré- as the first three letters perfect tense takes avoir – j'ai prévenu, tu as prévenu etc.						
tenir (to hold)	exactly the same pattern as venir but with t replacing v as the first letter perfect tense takes avoir – j'ai tenu, tu as tenu etc.						
boire (to drink)	je bois tu bois il boit nous buvons vous buvez ils boivent	je buvais tu buvais etc.	j'ai bu tu as bu etc.	je boirai tu boiras etc.	je boirais tu boirais etc.	bois! buvons! buvez!	il but ils burent
voir (to see)	je vois tu vois il voit nous voyons vous voyez ils voient	je voyais tu voyais etc.	j'ai vu tu as vu etc.	je verrai tu verras etc.	je verrais tu verrais etc.	vois! voyons! voyez!	il vit ils virent
écrire (to write)	j'écris tu écris il écrit nous écrivons vous écrivez ils écrivent	j'écrivais tu écrivais etc.	j'ai écrit tu as écrit etc.	j'écrirai tu écriras etc.	j'écrirais tu écrirais etc.	écris! écrivons! écrivez!	il écrit ils écrivirent
dire (to say, to tell)	je dis tu dis il dit nous disons vous dites ils disent	je disais tu disais etc.	j'ai dit tu as dit etc.	je dirai tu diras etc.	je dirais tu dirais etc.	dis! disons! dites!	il dit ils dirent
rire (to laugh)	je ris tu ris il rit nous rions vous riez ils rient	je riais tu riais etc.	j'ai ri tu as ri etc.	je rirai tu riras etc.	je rirais tu rirais etc.	ris! rions! riez!	il rit ils rirent
sourire (to smile)	exactly the same pattern as rire but with sou- as the first three letters je souris, tu souris etc.						
falloir (to be necessary)	il faut	il fallait	il a fallu	il faudra	il faudrait	—	il fallut
pleuvoir (to rain)	il pleut	il pleuvait	il a plu	il pleuvra	il pleuvrait	—	il plut

Index

The numbers in parenthesis refer to vocabulary sections.